BARBADOS

Marie Louise Elias

MARSHALL CAVENDISH
New York • London • Sydney

Reference edition reprinted 2000 by
Marshall Cavendish Corporation
99 White Plains Road
Tarrytown
New York 10591

© Times Media Private Limited 2000

Originated and designed by
Times Books International, an imprint of
Times Media Private Limited, a member of the
Times Publishing Group

Printed in Malaysia

Library of Congress Cataloging-in-Publication Data:

Elias, Marie Louise.
    Barbados / Marie Louise Elias.
        p. cm.—(Cultures of the World)
    Includes bibliographical references and index.
    Summary: Discusses the geography, history, government,
economy, people, and culture of Barbados, a small island nation in
the Caribbean.
    ISBN 0-7614-0976-9 (lib. bdg.)
    1. Barbados—Juvenile literature. [1. Barbados.] I. Title.
II. Series.
F2041.E45   2000
972.981—dc21   99–27594
                        CIP
                        AC

INTRODUCTION

A SMALL ISLAND NATION of great natural beauty, Barbados is part of the Lesser Antilles of the Caribbean. It has two distinct coastlines—the dramatic eastern coast with cliffs braced against thundering Atlantic breakers and the white sandy beaches and gentle waters of the west.

Culturally, Barbados is the result of over 300 years of British heritage, based on traditions that have produced a society recognized for its high level of education and its independent and democratic form of government. Political stability, a congenial climate, and a relaxed and fun-loving population combine to make Barbados one of the most attractive tourist destinations in the West Indies.

This book, part of the *Cultures of the World* series, examines this enchanting island surrounded by coral reefs and provides an insight into what makes Barbados's multiracial society so appealing to the rest of the world.

CONTENTS

Harvesting coconuts.

CONTENTS

Schoolboys line up outside their classroom in St. James.

GEOGRAPHY

BARBADOS IS A PEAR-SHAPED ISLAND, 21 miles (34 km) long and 14 miles (23 km) across at its widest, with a total land area of 166 square miles (430 square km). Approximately 300 miles (483 km) north of Venezuela and 100 miles (160 km) east of the Caribbean chain, it is, at 13 degrees 4 minutes north latitude and 59 degrees 37 minutes west longitude, the most easterly island of the West Indies.

TOPOGRAPHY

Geologically, Barbados is a relatively young island—it is only about a million years old. Unlike its neighbors to the west, which were formed by volcanic activity, it is composed of coral limestone accumulations built up on a ridge of submarine debris on the seabed, which collected sand and grit from the Orinoco River in South America.

Opposite: **Beach palms at Bathsheba on the eastern coast, facing the Atlantic Ocean.**

Left: **The rugged coastline at North Point in the parish of St. Lucy.**

Hackleton's Cliff in the east towers 1,000 feet (305 m) over the coast and is several miles long. It was formed when the eastern side of the island rose and tilted gently to the west. Waves pounding at the base of the cliff and raging waterfalls dislodged enormous boulders, which tumbled to the sea at Bathsheba.

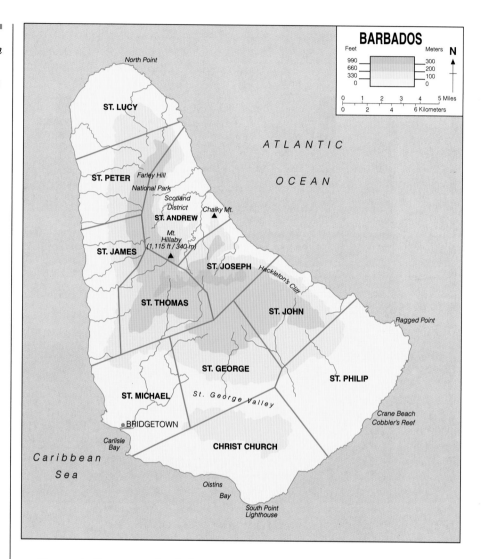

Tectonic forces pushed the coral out of the water, originally forming two small islands—today's central plateau around Mount Hillaby was once divided from the southern ridge of Christ Church by a shallow sea (St. George Valley). As it rose, the landmass, covered by a cap of coralstone, tilted, forming high cliffs to the east and a series of ridges and terraces to the west. Water permeating the island's porous limestone created underground streams, springs, and caverns. Surrounded by coral reefs, most of the island is relatively flat.

The west coast, with its white sandy beaches and calm blue waters, has become the center of Barbados's tourist industry. Most of the island's resorts and hotels are located there, as well as in the south. In contrast, high waves beat against the rocks and rugged cliffs of the less developed east coast. The north is the least populated region.

In the relatively hilly northeast, known as the Scotland District, erosion has removed much of the thick coral cover found on the rest of the island. Barbados's highest point, Mount Hillaby, rises to 1,115 feet (340 m) in the northcentral part of the island.

The island is divided into 11 parishes, or local administrative units, a legacy of the clergy's powerful influence in the past.

The jagged hilltops of Chalky Mount in St. Andrew parish consist of rocks striped in hues of pink, gray, and ocher, twisted and folded almost vertically during geological upheavals.

CLIMATE

Barbados has a tropical climate with daily temperatures ranging from 83°F (28°C) to 70°F (21°C) in January that only increase by a couple of degrees in July. The driest months are February to May with a mean humidity of 68%. The rest of the year the humidity averages between 74% and 79%. July is the wettest month, and annual rainfall averages 51 inches (130 cm).

HURRICANES The hurricane season in the Caribbean is from June to November, with hurricanes occurring most frequently in August and September. This region has one of the world's highest rates of hurricanes per year. Major hurricanes hit Barbados in 1667, 1731, 1780, and 1831, causing loss of life and extensive damage to property, but usually, these storms bypass the island to the north.

Hurricanes originate when high winds revolve in a counterclockwise direction around a center of lower barometric pressure. When the winds stay below 40 mph (65 kmph), it is known as a tropical depression. Winds between 40 and 75 mph (65 and 120 kmph) become a tropical storm. Only winds of at least 75 mph (120 kmph) qualify as hurricanes.

VEGETATION

Seeds of mangrove, sea coconuts, sea grape, sea spurge, sea bean, French cotton, and manchineel probably drifted to Barbados from South America hundreds of thousands of years ago. Once established, these plants stabilized the coastline. Coconuts, horse nicker, and lavender floated from Africa, while wind-borne seeds came with Sahara dust. Gradually a forest developed. Most of the native forests were cleared by early settlers for farming. The landscape now consists predominantly of sugarcane fields, pastures, and scrubland. The remaining woodlands are mainly found where gullies and cliffs make the land unsuitable for agriculture.

Only a few areas, such as Grenada Hall National Forest, have remained comparatively untouched. Turner's Hall Wood in the parish of St. Andrew is a remnant of the dense tropical forest that covered the island at the time

Opposite: **Many of the larger churches around the island have the words "hurricane shelter" painted either on a wall or on their gates.**

Left: **Rich agricultural land in St. George Valley in the south of Barbados.**

Legend has it that the grapefruit was first developed in Barbados in the 18th century by a natural cross-pollination between the shaddock (the Barbadian name for the Malaysian pomelo) and the sweet orange from the Far East. Originally known as "forbidden fruit," its name was changed to grapefruit because it grows in grape-like clusters.

THE BAOBAB

The baobab tree (*Adansonia digitata*), also known as the "monkey bread tree," is said to have been brought to Barbados around 1738 from Africa. It takes 15 adults joined with outstretched arms to encircle one such tree in Queen's Park in Bridgetown.

of the first settlement in 1627. Fine examples of silk cotton, sand box, trumpet tree, cabbage palm, and the indigenous macaw palm grow there. Other trees common to Barbados include the bearded fig tree (*Ficus citrofolia*), casuarina, white cedar, poinciana, locust, and mahogany.

Welchman Hall Gully, a deep ravine planted in the 1860s, is well-known for its groves of citrus and spice-bearing trees as well as many other rare trees.

ANIMAL LIFE

A few introduced species of mammals such as mongooses, green monkeys (*Cercopithecus aethiops*), hares, mice, and rats can be found in the wild. A nonpoisonous and rarely seen grass snake (*Liophis perfuscus*) is only found on Barbados, but there are other harmless blind snakes, whistling frogs, lizards, red-footed tortoises, and eight species of bats. Hawksbill turtles lay their eggs on the sandy beaches and the leatherback turtle is an occasional nester.

GREEN MONKEYS

Introduced as pets from West Africa some 350 years ago, green monkeys quickly found their way into the wild where, with no predators, they multiplied rapidly. Because monkeys have the same food preferences as humans, they have always been considered pests by farmers, who can lose up to a third of their banana, mango, and papaya crops to them.

Today the island's monkey population is estimated at between 5,000 and 10,000. As they are neither rare nor endangered, either on the island or worldwide, the government has long encouraged the hunting of monkeys. The first bounties were introduced as early as the late 1600s, but in 1975, the Ministry of Agriculture introduced a bounty of Bds$5 for every monkey tail. After the Barbados Primate Research Center was founded in 1982, a more enticing reward of Bds$50 was offered for each monkey captured alive and delivered unharmed to the center. As a result, monkeys are now usually trapped rather than shot.

Although more than 180 species of birds have been sighted on Barbados, most are migrating shorebirds and waders that stop over from North America on their way to winter feeding grounds in South America. Only 28 species actually nest on Barbados, including wood doves, blackbirds, banana-quits, guinea fowl, cattle egrets, herons, finches, and three kinds of hummingbirds.

The seas around Barbados abound with more than 50 varieties of fish, providing a source of livelihood for many people. Surface-dwelling fish of the open seas (pelagic fish) are found five to 25 miles (eight to 40 km) offshore. Dolphins, kingfish, billfish, sharks, flying fish, and bonito fall into this category. Big game fish include blue marlin—one weighing 910 pounds (410 kg) was caught off Barbados in 1996—white marlin, sailfish, and tuna. Coral reefs are home to a rich marine life, including ning-nings, velvets, lobsters, moray eels, octopuses, and gorgonias.

A red-footed tortoise in St. Peter.

MAIN TOWNS

BRIDGETOWN in the parish of St. Michael is the island's capital and commercial center. It has a population of approximately 100,000, and was founded in 1628 on Carlisle Bay, the island's only natural harbor.

Bridgetown's main street includes some restored colonial buildings. The Careenage, an inlet now lined with recreational boats, cuts into the heart of the city. Interisland schooners carrying fresh produce and other goods docked here for 300 years, while sailing ships sought harbor in the outer basin or were careened (turned sideways to scrape and clean the hull) in the inner basin. Before the construction of Bridgetown Harbor in 1961, large vessels and dreadnoughts anchored in Carlisle Bay.

A bird's eye view of Bridgetown.

Independence Arch, which commemorates Bajan—a term used to describe the people of Barbados or Barbadians—independence is at the south side of Chamberlain Bridge, which crosses the Careenage to Trafalgar Square. This square marks the bustling center of the city's political, financial, commercial, and seafaring life. On Remembrance Day, military parades fill the square and poppy wreaths are laid at the Cenotaph, an obelisk monument honoring World War I dead erected in 1925.

HOLETOWN is in the sophisticated parish of St. James. It was originally called St. James Town by the first English settlers who landed here in 1625 aboard the *Olive Blossom* and claimed the island in the name of King James I of England. An obelisk monument and mural running along the main road in the town center commemorates this event, but the date on the monument, July 1605, is two decades early.

A recent development has incorporated the monument, post office, and police station into a compound reminiscent of those early days.

SPEIGHTSTOWN in the parish of St. Peter, named after a 1639 member of parliament, William Speight, was once dubbed Little Bristol because it was the main shipping line to Bristol in England when sugar was Barbados's mainstay.

A quiet place, slightly off the beaten track, it is the only town on the island to retain many of its original small streets lined with simple two-story houses, some of which have Georgian-style balconies and overhanging galleries.

OISTINS in the parish of Christ Church is the center of the island's fishing industry. It has a large and bustling fish market open daily as long as the catch—dolphin, shark, barracuda, snapper, and flying fish—keeps arriving. The government has built a Bds$10 million fisheries terminal to encourage modernization of the fishing industry. The growing number of deep sea fishing boats, which have replaced smaller vessels, make good use of the ice machines in the terminal.

Speightstown is the main town in the north.

HISTORY

UNLIKE SOME OF ITS CARIBBEAN NEIGHBORS, Barbados was not discovered by Christopher Columbus, the renowned Italian explorer in the service of the Spanish king. The first Europeans to note the island on their maps were the Portuguese, but it was not until early in the 17th century that Barbados was claimed by English explorers.

THE FIRST BARBADIANS

The ancestors of Barbados's first inhabitants came from South America—first the Arawaks from Bolivia and Peru who came via Venezuela, and much later, the Caribs from Brazil via Guyana and Trinidad.

The Arawaks were skilled farmers and fishermen and accomplished in the ceramic crafts, which they traded among other communities throughout the Caribbean area. They were short, olive-skinned, and handsome. Their

Opposite: **The Gun Hill military signal station in St. George, now preserved as a historic site, once served as a communications point for British forces on the island.**

Left: **Old cannons in the Garrison in Bridgetown.**

Barbados may have been named after the bearded fig trees found on the island.

villages, sited in sheltered bays with fresh water, were strung along the coastline in areas where the fishing grounds were good, particularly at the northeastern tip of the island. The Arawaks fished and farmed, cultivating cassava, potatoes, and corn. They made *casareep* ("ka-sa-REEP") from grated, ground cassava, a unique flavoring still used in Caribbean cuisine today.

These early settlers lived harmoniously in relative isolation in Barbados until about A.D. 1250, when the Caribs, a taller, stronger tribe, arrived in sturdy boats hollowed out from single logs. Practicing cannibalism, they were more aggressive and quickly subdued their predecessors.

Nevertheless, Carib settlements disappeared during the early 16th century when Spanish conquistadores began raiding the island regularly for slaves to work in the sugar estates and mines in Hispaniola. Those who managed to evade the slave-raids escaped to neighboring Windward Islands, where they could consolidate their defenses against the Spaniards. Barbados was effectively abandoned by its early Native American settlers because the island's lack of mountains made it difficult for them to defend themselves from raiders.

In 1536 Portuguese explorer Pedro a Campos, on his way to Brazil, claimed the island was uninhabited. He is said to have given the island its name of Los Barbados ("the Bearded Ones"), presumably after the fig trees with long-hanging aerial roots that have a marked, beard-like resemblance. Barbados's name is thus Portuguese in origin.

ARRIVAL OF THE ENGLISH

When Captain John Powell landed on Barbados in May 1625 and claimed it for King James I of England, all he found was a flourishing herd of wild hogs, descendants of those left behind by the Portuguese. The first English settlement was established in Jamestown (now Holetown) in February 1627 when a party of 80 settlers and 10 black slaves, captured en route, landed on the island.

Financed by William Courteen & Associates, the pioneer colonists were employees rather than freehold farmers. They owned neither land nor stock. Helped by white indentured servants and meeting no armed resistance, these settlers were able to concentrate on the immediate task of planting crops and establishing trade systems. Because other English settlements in the West Indies were hampered by continuous native opposition, Barbados quickly surpassed them all, both in population growth and commercial activity.

THE CREATION OF PLANTOCRACY

In 1639 Governor Henry Hawley established a House of Assembly. The land tenure system was changed and land was issued to colonists in return for a quit rent of 40 pounds (18 kg) of tobacco annually. Only men with large sums of capital could afford to become substantial landholders, so a society dominated by a small, landed elite developed. Land was effectively allocated mostly to colonists with known financial and social connections in England. English law and tradition took hold quickly, and the island became known as "Little England."

The first English settlement on Barbados was named for King James I (ruled 1603–25).

Dripstones made of coral limestone were once used to filter drinking water taken from wells, ponds, or springs before piped water provided a more reliable supply.

THE FIRST CROPS Barbados was described as a colony "built on smoke" because at first tobacco was its only export. By 1631, however, planters were cultivating cotton, which was fetching high prices in London. Boom conditions prevailed until 1639 when the London market was oversupplied with cotton. Prices fell sharply and the colonists had to find a new crop.

INDENTURED SERVANTS The production of tobacco, cotton, and indigo relied heavily on a labor force of British indentured servants. More than half the whites who came to Barbados during the 1630s and 1640s were indentured servants, contracted to serve their employers for periods of five years (if over 21 years old) or up to seven (if under 21) in return for passage to the colony and subsistence on arrival.

Indentured servants were little more than slaves. They could be bought or sold, even gambled away. They were not permitted to leave their plantations without a pass signed by their master. Their contracts gave them certain rights, such as the receipt of adequate food, clothing, and shelter, and the right to complain to local magistrates of mistreatment by their masters.

Since planters believed they could treat their "property" in whatever way they wished within the limits of the "customs of the country," these rights were seldom exercised. The descendants of these Scots, Irish, and Welsh indentured servants would later be known as "red legs," the name coming from the sunburned skin on their kilt-exposed legs.

INTRODUCTION OF SUGARCANE

Sugarcane was first brought to the island in 1637 by a Dutchman who had learned how to grow and process it in Brazil. Defeated by the Portuguese in Brazil, the Dutch needed a market for their sugar-making machinery and their slave trade. Dutch merchants, many of them Jewish, were not allowed by law and custom to contract white servants, so they encouraged their thriving African slave trade by helping struggling English colonists with capital and technology.

By 1645 Barbados was flourishing. Five years later it was described as the richest spot in the New World. Barbadians dominated the sugar industry in the early years as the wealth of the planter class increased. Large sugarcane estates were formed by combining smaller ones that did not have access to sufficient capital.

During the next 15 years the number of landholders declined substantially. Although they were less than 10% of the island's population, the elite plantocracy dominated public life and civic organizations and made sure that only white, Anglo-Saxon Anglicans were allowed any political or legal power. Some of them received knighthoods or baronetcies in the second half of the century.

A sketch of an early sugar plantation. Producing sugar was so profitable that planters preferred buying expensive imported food to growing food on their own land.

INTRODUCTION OF SLAVES

Large numbers of slaves had to be brought in to work the sugar fields, mills, boiling houses, and distilleries. The plantations could not have existed without these slaves who came to Barbados from West Africa. There were many different ethnic groups, speaking different languages.

A woodcut of a slave ship.

They were housed in floorless huts, given meager food, and forced to work 12 hours a day, six days a week. Skilled slaves such as carpenters, blacksmiths, and tailors fared better, and domestic slaves were more trusted and better treated than field workers.

FIRST SLAVE ACTS During the sugar boom, the slave population of 5,680 in 1645 rose to 60,000 by 1684, outnumbering the whites by three to one. Acts were passed to control this vast labor force. The 1688 Act declared slaves to be "real estate," which legally tied them to specific plantations and meant that they could neither own property nor give evidence in court against whites.

Slaves could not leave their plantation without a ticket signed by their master, nor were they allowed to beat drums, blow horns, or use other loud instruments.

ABORTED SLAVE REBELLIONS From the very beginning, Africans resisted their enslavement in Barbados. Plantation houses were built to incorporate defenses against slave attacks. The first recorded incident was a small-scale uprising in 1649. However, in 1675 a planned revolt by African-born slaves, involving a large number of plantations across the island, was discovered and the ringleaders were arrested and executed.

A more widespread conspiracy that involved plans for slaves to form themselves into four regiments of foot soldiers and two mounted regiments with the intention of bringing the entire island under black control, was exposed in 1692. Of the 200 to 300 slaves who were arrested and brought to trial, 92 were executed.

The black population, however, was rapidly becoming Creole as opposed to African-born. No other attempted rebellions were recorded in Barbados between 1702 and 1815, not only because the white community established and maintained a powerful island-wide system for the control of slaves with dozens of forts strung out along the coast, but also for the following reasons listed by William Dickson, a leading literary authority on 18th century slavery in Barbados:

A sketch of slaves harvesting sugarcane.

"1. The colony is the oldest sugar producer in the region and the majority of the slaves are Creole; these slaves are less aggressive in their responses to enslavement than African-born slaves.

2. These slaves are more exposed to the Christian religion than in the other islands, which has a pacifying effect upon them.

3. There is a large white female population, which unlike elsewhere tempers white male aggression and produces a more civil social outlook.

4. The colony's topography and geography are less conducive to 'marronage' (fugitive slaves) than other West Indian islands.

5. Planters grant more socioeconomic concessions to their slaves than their counterparts in other islands; hence slaves appear to have more 'libertie.'

6. Because of the size and organization of the white community, the day-to-day discipline and control of slaves is more effective.

7. There is far less absentee landlordship than elsewhere, and the social culture and outlook of the white elite are more conducive to social stability."

THE 18TH CENTURY

During the 18th century, Barbados languished. Competition from islands such as Jamaica and St. Kitts intensified and the price of sugar fell sharply. War with France and the American War of Independence caused trade between Barbados and the British colonies in America to plummet, cutting off food supplies for slaves and material for the sugar industry. Food shortages became so serious that the poor died in the streets.

Barbados also suffered several other calamities. Yellow fever in 1703 caused many deaths. A hurricane in 1731 wreaked widespread damage and was followed by a drought two years later. An even more destructive hurricane struck in 1780, destroying crops and killing over 2,000 people.

Recognizing Barbados's strategic location, the English used the island for a multi-island defense center. British regiments were stationed in

A milk-white limestone lion, sculpted in 1868, guards the road to the Gun Hill signal station.

26

imposing arched brick buildings in the Garrison in Bridgetown. By 1795 Barbados had 22 forts, 450 guns, and a series of elevated signal stations that could relay signals to alert the entire island within minutes of sighting an aggressor to the north or south.

The victory of Lord Admiral Nelson at Trafalgar in 1805 and the military success of English troops in the West Indies stabilized sugar markets, and Nelson was hailed as a hero.

THE END OF SLAVERY

The abolition of the slave trade in 1807 caused the plantocracy little concern, even though Barbadian blacks (especially the artisans and domestics who were better informed and considered themselves closer to freedom) had become more aggressive after Haitian revolutionaries declared independence in 1804.

Lord Nelson's crucial victory over the combined French and Spanish fleets at the Battle of Trafalgar not only saved Britain from invasion—it also ensured the supremacy of British sea power for another century.

LORD HORATIO NELSON

The bronze statue of Lord Nelson, who sailed into Barbados in 1805 a few months before dying at the Battle of Trafalgar, was erected in Bridgetown in 1813, two decades before its larger London counterpart. Over the years the statue has been the subject of controversy among the islanders, some of whom feel it embraces the island's colonial past too closely. In the 1970s the Mighty Gabby, a leading calypso singer, had a popular song called "Take Down Nelson," suggesting replacing Nelson with a Bajan man.

BUSSA'S REBELLION OF 1816

Commemorated by the Emancipation Statue, which was unveiled in 1985 at the border between St. Michael and St. George parishes, this rebellion was the result of a misunderstanding. In 1815 Britain passed a bill declaring that all slaves in the West Indies had to be registered. Believing this bill was a threat to their right of self-government, the Barbadian House of Assembly rejected it. The slaves thought the bill was not to register them but intended to free them. It was the unfulfilled expectation of freedom that sparked the rebellion.

An African-born slave called Bussa was the primary leader. Rebel contingents assembled at his plantation in St. Philip where sugarcane fields were set alight. The revolt spread but was eventually suppressed by the British militia. Bussa is believed to have died in battle at the head of his contingent during the final showdown.

In 1833 the Emancipation Act was passed into law and took effect on August 1, 1834. All slaves under the age of 6 were unconditionally emancipated. Slaves over the age of 6 were freed, but had to continue to serve their former owners as unpaid apprentices for six years. This was intended to give the slaves time to adjust gradually to freedom and the slave owners the opportunity to reorganize their plantations on the basis of free, wage laborers.

But instead of improving working conditions for the former slaves, the act had the opposite effect. The planters' attitude to their workforce hardened, and workers become sullen and unproductive. When the planters abandoned all responsibility for infants, workers had to struggle to provide for their children and many of the 14,000 children who had been freed in 1834 joined the ranks of the destitute in the colony. It soon became clear that the apprenticeship system was a farce, and on August 1, 1838, all slaves were fully emancipated, two years ahead of schedule.

THE 20TH CENTURY

Subsidized sugar beet production in Europe caused a crisis for Barbados's sugar industry during the mid-1890s, and many indebted estates were sold to the urban merchant class. Thus bolstered by the wealth of the merchant families, the plantocracy entered the 20th century secure in their ability to rule in the difficult times ahead.

The British government's growing concern for the welfare of the working class found little support among the Barbadian planters, who remained determined to keep their plantation labor in line and restrict the education of black children to discourage them from seeking employment outside agriculture. Although ownership of their own piece of land was the ambition of nearly every plantation worker, very few succeeded in obtaining freehold.

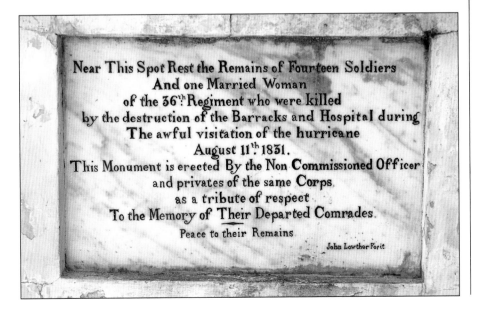

A memorial to victims of the great hurricane of 1831.

PANAMA MAN The resumption of construction on the Panama Canal by the United States in 1904 provided male Barbadian workers with an opportunity to escape from plantation work. Planters, unconcerned by the migration of part of their labor force, then employed women to do men's work at lower wages.

Some 20,000 men emigrated to Panama. Former field hands returning from Panama had enough money to buy land, open shops, learn a craft, or acquire education for clerical or business professions. A slump in sugar prices forced indebted planters to sell some of their plantations in small lots to these "Panama men," and the pattern of land ownership changed significantly.

Although many of the workers returning from Panama were able to achieve a better quality of life, for the majority of the working class, conditions deteriorated.

BLACK POWER A combination of education, societies for the working class, and the Barbados Labor Union (formed in 1919) provided the background for the development of a radical political movement in Barbados, abetted by Marcus Garvey's pan-Caribbean and international "black power" movement.

During the 1930s, a rapidly growing population, the rising cost of living, and dissatisfaction with wages fixed at the equivalent of 30 US cents a day sparked spontaneous street riots in Barbados. Fourteen people were killed and 47 wounded in protests in 1937. The rioting spurred Grantley Adams to found the Barbados Labor Party (BLP) in 1938. During the 1942 House of Assembly session, Adams led a fight for reforms that allowed more people to qualify to vote, increased direct taxation, and established a workmen's compensation program. Adams became the island's first premier in 1954.

INDEPENDENCE As leader of a discontented BLP left-wing, Errol Barrow felt that Adams was too close to the governor and not close enough to the masses. He left the BLP in 1951 and founded the Democratic Labor Party the following year. Barbados gained internal self-government in 1961 and became an independent nation within the Commonwealth on November 30, 1966. Errol Barrow was the first prime minister.

Above: **Barbados welcomes its head of state, Queen Elizabeth II, on a official visit.**

Left: **Working on the Panama Canal was dangerous, but many Barbadians were attracted by the money they could earn.**

GOVERNMENT

UNIQUE AMONG THE ISLANDS OF THE CARIBBEAN, Barbados was ruled by Britain for an unbroken stretch of more than 300 years. Today it still maintains strong links with Britain. This has helped to create a foundation of stability in a country made up of different races and creeds.

CHARTER OF BARBADOS

The English Parliament, after the execution of King Charles I in 1649, decided planters in Barbados were rebels and launched an operation to subdue the colony. A fleet under Sir George Asycue blockaded the island until early 1652, when the colonists accepted the terms offered by Asycue's delegation and signed articles of capitulation, agreeing to recognize the rule of parliament and its governor in return for continued self-government, free trade, and the restoration of confiscated properties.

Opposite: **A member of the Barbados Defense Force.**

Left: **Independence Arch in Bridgetown commemorates the country's independence on November 30, 1966.**

This formed the basis for the Charter of Barbados, which guaranteed government by a governor and a freely-elected assembly as well as freedom from taxation without local consent. When the monarchy was restored in England in 1660, this charter provided Barbados with a greater measure of independence from the English monarchy than any of the other British colonies.

THE CONSTITUTION

Barbados's political system is a constitutional monarchy, with Queen Elizabeth II as head of state, represented by the governor-general, Sir Clifford Husbands. The constitution dates from 1966 and provides for a system of parliamentary government on the British model, with a prime minister and cabinet drawn from and responsible to the legislature, which consists of a Senate and a House of Assembly.

Once the town hall and then a prison, the Law Courts building in Bridgetown is a handsome Georgian building. It has survived two great hurricanes and several fires.

THE SENATE AND HOUSE OF ASSEMBLY

The Senate consists of 21 members appointed by the governor-general, 12 on the advice of the prime minister, two on the advice of the leader of the opposition, and the rest on the basis of wider consultations. The House of Assembly, which dates back to 1951, has 28 members elected by universal suffrage. The voting age is 18 years.

The legislature has a maximum life of five years and can be dissolved anytime during this period. The governor-general appoints both the prime minister—on the basis of support in the House of Assembly—and the leader of the opposition. Cabinet ministers are also appointed by the governor-general, on the advice of the prime minister.

Parliament House in Bridgetown is the seat of the country's Senate and House of Assembly.

POLITICAL PARTIES AND MAJOR POLITICIANS

THE BARBADOS LABOR PARTY (moderate, left-of-center) won the first general election in 1951. It was formed in 1938 by Grantley Adams, who became premier in 1954 when ministerial government was established.

GRANTLEY ADAMS A lawyer who had won the Barbados Scholarship to Oxford University in 1918, Grantley Adams became the most important figure in preindependence politics. He rose to prominence through his testimony before the British Moyne Commission investigating regional disturbances in the late 1930s, claiming that the riots were caused mainly by economic distress.

A statue of Grantley Adams in Bridgetown is flanked by portraits of other political leaders.

Elected to the House of Assembly in 1940 and president-general of the Barbados Workers Union in 1941, he became leader of the government in 1946. In 1951, in the first election conducted under universal adult suffrage with no property qualifications, the BLP won 16 of the 24 seats, thus gaining a majority. Adams was knighted in 1952. He is the only person ever to hold the office of prime minister of the West Indies Federation, which was dissolved in 1962 when Jamaica and Trinidad and Tobago opted for independence.

Under his leadership, Barbados was transformed from an oligarchy into a democracy based on universal suffrage. A wide range of social reforms was introduced, and major construction projects such as Bridgetown's deep water harbor started.

THE DEMOCRATIC LABOR PARTY (moderate, left-of-center) was formed in 1955. When full internal self-government was achieved in 1961, the party won the general election under its leader Errol Barrow, who became the first prime minister when full independence was gained in 1966.

Errol Barrow, prime minister of Barbados 1966–76 and 1986–87.

ERROL BARROW Barrow served in the British Royal Air Force during World War II and subsequently studied law in London. He returned to Barbados in 1950, joined the BLP, and was elected to the House in 1951. He became the leader of a discontented BLP left-wing, which felt that Adams was too close to the governor and not giving enough attention to the workers.

Tom Adams led Barbados into the 1980s, but died of a heart attack in 1985 while in office.

In 1954 Barrow left the BLP. The following year he founded the Democratic Labor Party, which he led for the next 32 years. He gained the support of sugar workers demanding higher wages, and his party won the 1961 elections. Between 1961 and 1966, the DLP replaced the Legislative Council with a Senate appointed by the governor, increased workers' benefits, instituted a program for industrialization, and expanded free education.

The DLP won the November 1966 elections and Barrow became the first prime minister when Barbados gained its independence on November 30, 1966. Other significant achievements during his period in office include the introduction of free secondary and university education and the lowering of the voting age to 18.

The BLP was reelected in 1976 under Grantley Adams' son Tom, who died suddenly in 1985 and was succeeded by Bernard St. John. The following year, the DLP, led by Errol Barrow, returned to power with 24 of the 27 seats in the House of Assembly. Errol Barrow died suddenly in 1987 and was succeeded by the deputy prime minister, Erskine Lloyd Sandiford.

A new opposition party, the National Democratic Party (center), was formed in 1989 by Richard Haynes, a former minister of finance in Sandiford's cabinet. Nevertheless, the DPL, under Sandiford, won the general election in 1991. In September 1994 Owen Seymour Arthur became the fifth prime minister after leading the BLP to victory in 19 of the 28 seats in the House of Assembly, securing 48% of the total votes. The DLP won eight seats and the NLP one.

NATIONAL SECURITY

During the 17th and 18th centuries, Barbados was an important military base for the British to protect their interests in the Caribbean. The many antiquated cannons still found on the island are a reminder of those turbulent times when Barbados held a vital role in regional power.

Today, Barbados is a peaceful island with little crime and no longer requires a large military force. The Barbados Defense Force, established in 1978, has a strength of:

500   armed forces personnel
110   navy (coastguard)
430   reserve force

Barbados also has a police force of about 1,000, who are mainly involved in controlling traffic.

FOREIGN RELATIONS

Both the DLP and the BLP are committed to maintaining free enterprise and alignment with the United States. In 1972 the DLP government reestablished diplomatic relations with Cuba, while still maintaining cordial relations with the United States. In 1979, in a move described by prime minister Tom Adams as an act of "East Caribbean defense cooperation," the BLP administration dispatched troops to St. Vincent to help maintain order when St. Vincent police were deployed in containing an uprising on the Grenadines' Union Island.

In 1983 the BLP government participated in the US invasion of Grenada. This action, however, strained relations with Trinidad, which claimed that the operation was undertaken without properly consulting all members of the Caribbean Community.

Banners around the island welcome the president of Guyana on a state visit.

Owen Arthur favors establishing a new partnership between the Caribbean and the United States to secure peace, prosperity, and stability in the region. During the Cold War, US policy saw the region primarily as a transshipment area for illicit drugs intended for the US market. Arthur believes that integration into the global economy is the best option for the Caribbean nations and has declared that the region is committed to negotiations for a Free Trade Area of the Americas (FTAA) by 2005.

Barbados is a member of international organizations such as the United Nations (UN), the Organization of American States (OAS), the Caribbean Community (CARICOM), the Commonwealth, and the Inter-American Development Bank (IDB). Countries with diplomatic representation in Barbados include Brazil, Canada, the People's Republic of China, Colombia, Costa Rica, the United Kingdom, the United States, and Venezuela.

The Commonwealth is a free association of over 50 independent nations, representing over a quarter of the world's population. Most members were formerly British colonies. Barbados was admitted into the Commonwealth in 1966 when it gained independence.

ORGANIZATION OF AMERICAN STATES

The Organization of American States (OAS) was first established as the International Union of American Republics at a meeting in Washington, D.C., in 1890. The main objectives of the OAS include strengthening the peace and security of the American continent; ensuring the peaceful settlement of disputes among member states; and promoting economic, social, and cultural development through cooperative action.

Most countries in North, South, and Central America as well as the Caribbean, including the United States, are members of the OAS. A notable exception, however, is Cuba—its membership has been suspended since 1962. The OAS is headquartered in Washington, D.C., and has an annual budget of about US$100 million contributed by member governments. Every member nation has one vote, and unlike the United Nations, no country has veto power.

ECONOMY

THE ECONOMY OF BARBADOS is based on four main sectors—tourism, offshore financial services, agriculture including fishing, and manufacturing.

TOURISM

The tourist industry had its origins in the years just before World War I, catering for winter visitors from North America and the United Kingdom as well as visitors from Latin America, particularly Brazil. The colony owed much of its increasing prosperity to such visitors, but the tourist industry remained subordinate to sugar until the 1970s, when it nudged sugar into second place.

Tourism now accounts for nearly 50% of the island's GNP and is the major source for foreign exchange. It also provides employment for a large percentage of the labor force.

Opposite and left: **Tourism employs more than 10% of the workforce and brings in half the country's foreign exchange. Visitors from the United States and the United Kingdom make up more than half of all tourist arrivals in Barbados.**

OFFSHORE FINANCIAL SERVICES

Barbados has been actively encouraging international offshore companies, such as banks, insurers, trusts, and shipping registration companies, to register in the country by exempting them from capital gains tax and estate duty. Expansion plans for the financial services sector include new legislation, marketing and promotion, and the negotiation of more double taxation agreements with other countries.

AGRICULTURE

Although the government has embarked on a policy of agricultural diversification to increase the production of fruits, vegetables, poultry, and meat, sugarcane is still the main cash crop and makes a large contribution to the island's export earnings.

SUGARCANE (*Saccharum officinarum*) is a giant, thick, perennial grass cultivated for its sweet sap. The plant grows in clumps of solid stalks and has graceful, sword-

AN EARLY TOURIST

In 1751, more than two decades before he became the first president of the United States, George Washington came to Barbados with his half-brother Lawrence, who suffered from tuberculosis and was hoping that the tropical climate would prove therapeutic. Unfortunately, George contracted smallpox while on Barbados, which left his face permanently scarred, and Lawrence died the following year. The Barbados trip was the only overseas journey George Washington ever made.

shaped leaves. Mature canes can grow to 10 to 26 feet (3 to 8 m) tall and one to two inches (2.5 to 5 cm) in diameter. The color of the stalk ranges from almost white to yellow to deep green, purple, red, or violet.

About 30% of sugarcane sap is sucrose. During harvesting, the cane stalks are stripped of leaves and trimmed for easier handling. In the factory, the stalks are washed and cut into short lengths or shredded. The sugar is removed from the canes by a diffusion process, where the sugar is separated from the finely-cut stalks by dissolving them in hot water, or by milling, where the juice is squeezed from the stalks by pressing them between heavy rollers. In the later process, the rollers are arranged in sets of three, each set exerting a greater pressure than the last. Water is sprayed on the stalks as they pass through the rollers to help dissolve additional juice. The waste material remaining after the rolling is called bagasse.

Above: **A banana plantation in St. Joseph.**

Opposite: **The Central Bank of Barbados was established in 1972. Barbados's importance as an offshore banking center is growing, and the sector is an important source of foreign earnings for the country.**

Workers harvest sugar-cane. Sugar still plays a major role in the economy, although it has since been overtaken by tourism.

The acidic liquid extracted from cane is dark gray or greenish and contains impurities that need to be clarified by the use of chemicals. Milk of lime (a mixture of calcium hydroxide and water) is added to the juice, which is immediately heated to the boiling point and then run into settling tanks where the precipitated matter is separated from the clear juice. To produce white sugar directly from the cane juice, sulfur dioxide and sometimes phosphoric acid are added to the juice before the milk of lime.

The juice is evaporated into a thick syrup and then concentrated by vacuum boiling in several stages. The vacuum allows the mixture to boil at a relatively low temperature to prevent scorching of the syrup. It is boiled until sugar crystallizes out of the liquid, forming a mixture known as massecuite. Centrifugal machines (perforated hollow cylinders that revolve rapidly) separate the raw sugar crystals from the massecuite.

The Portvale sugar factory in St. James parish is one of the largest cane-grinding factories on the island. A by-product of the sugarcane industry is rum.

THE MORGAN LEWIS SUGAR MILL

This huge stone mill is the largest and only complete sugar windmill surviving in the Caribbean. It is typical of the wind-driven mills that crushed sugarcane for two centuries and produced the commodity that once made Barbados one of Britain's most valuable possessions in the Americas. The machinery that ground the cane is intact, but the canvas sails that caught the wind and turned the grinding mechanism are no longer on the arms.

FISHING

The fishing industry, which had been in decline since the mid-1980s, has improved in recent years. New and expanded facilities have been constructed at the main fishing port of Oistins, and increasingly, small boats are being replaced by larger and more powerful boats with large ice storage chests that enable fishermen to stay at sea longer. More than 700 fishing vessels are used during the peak fishing season.

Closer inshore, reef fish are caught by simple lines from open boats or trapped in cage-like fishpots. Along the shore, nets of varying sizes are cast for fish ranging from fray and sprat to pilcher and grubbing.

A flying fish vendor in Bridgetown.

TRAINING FOR FISHERMEN   The Fisheries Department conducts introductory training programs to teach fishermen to operate fishing vessels. It also plans to acquire a simulated wheelhouse, marine engines, and possibly its own fishing vessel, which can be used not only for training but also for marine science and exploratory and experimental fishing.

FLYING FISH   Despite its name, the flying fish does not fly. It can, however, glide considerable distances by using its four "wings" (its pectoral and ventral fins). Although 13 species of flying fish are found in the waters surrounding Barbados, only one species, *Hyrundichthys affinis*, is caught commercially. In May when the fish spawn, they can be scooped aboard by using a dip net. Flying fish account for 60% of all fish caught by commercial fishermen, and Barbados has often been called "The Land of the Flying Fish."

Traditional fishermen in Oistins. The government is helping fishermen to upgrade to larger boats that can fish in waters further from the island.

A rum bottling plant in Bridgetown.

MANUFACTURING

Manufacturing contributes some 7% to Barbados's GDP and provides jobs for about 10% of the workforce. Electronic components, clothing, cement, furniture, medical supplies, and processed food are some of the products manufactured in Barbados.

MINING

The limestone that covers over two-thirds of the island contains few impurities and is well-suited for the manufacture of cement and the production of slaked lime for the iron, steel, and chemical industries. Some limestone locations produce what is locally called "soft stone," traditionally used in the building industry for making blocks.

Sand is also mined for the production of green and amber glass and for the building industry. Modern houses in Barbados are often built from cement or sandstone blocks.

THE ARAWAK CEMENT COMPANY

Shut down for six years, the Arawak Cement Company plant was reopened in 1997. It is now back to 80% capacity, having undergone a comprehensive restructuring program. At full capacity, the plant can produce 6,500 tons (6,000 metric tons) of cement a week. To protect the environment, the use of a new environment-friendly fuel is being pioneered. Orimulsion, a low-emission fuel, is also used to fire the kiln.

FOREIGN TRADE

Sugar and its by-products, rum and molasses, together with electrical/electronic components, clothing, and chemicals, are the country's chief exports. Main imports include machinery, food and beverages, fuels, and automobiles. The United States, the United Kingdom, and Trinidad and Tobago are Barbados's top trading partners.

ENERGY

Nearly half the country's energy needs are supplied from domestic oil and natural gas production. There is a refinery in Bridgetown.

Production of petroleum started at Woodbourne in St. Philip in 1972. The oil fields were nationalized in 1982, and a national petroleum

CURRENCY

The Barbados dollar is tied to the US dollar at a fixed rate of Bds$2 to US$1. Other foreign currencies fluctuate daily against that standard. Barbadian notes come in the following denominations: Bds$2 (blue), Bds$5 (green), Bds$10 (brown), Bds$20 (purple), Bds$50 (orange), and Bds$100 (gray). Coins are in denominations of Bds$1, and 1, 5, 10, and 25 cents.

Barbados has about four million barrels of oil reserves. Stepped-up exploration, if successful, could boost this figure considerably.

corporation was set up to implement public policy on crude oil and natural gas production. In a typical year, the island's more than 100 wells produce about 480,000 barrels of crude oil. In late 1996 the Barbados National Oil Company signed an agreement with a US company to step up exploration activity, with the aim of making the country self-sufficient in energy.

Solar radiation levels, estimated at 3,200 calories per square inch (500 calories per square cm) per day, are among the highest in the world. Solar energy has been commercially available since 1974, providing a substitute for natural gas and imported energy. Over 20,000 houses in Barbados have solar panels on their roofs. A wind turbine at Lamberts in St. Lucy also provides electricity to the Barbados Light & Power Company.

Bagasse, a by-product of the sugar industry, is an important source of biomass fuel and is mainly used to meet the energy requirements of sugarcane processing.

Drilling for oil in St. Philip.

TRANSPORTATION

A network of major highways, all beginning at Bridgetown, spans the island. Driving time from Bridgetown to the east coast has been greatly reduced with the completion of the trans-insular highway, which cuts across the island. Public transportation is excellent, with government-operated Transport Board buses, privately-run minibuses, and individually-owned minivan cabs. Minibuses are perhaps the most popular form of transportation, as they are usually better maintained than government buses and less crowded than minivans. Virtually any place on the island can be reached by public bus as buses cover all the extensive paved road network on regular schedules.

Public transportation is comprehensive and inexpensive.

Barbados's only international airport, the Grantley Adams International Airport, is located 7 miles (11 km) east of Bridgetown. It is served by several international airlines, including British West Indian Airlines, British Airways, American Airlines, and Air Canada. Miami is about three hours away by air and New York five hours.

Bridgetown's new deep-sea harbor is a port of call for British, European, and American cruise lines. The number of cruise ship passengers arriving in Barbados has been increasing steadily. By 1996, passenger arrivals had exceeded half a million, nearly double the local population.

A train service, now discontinued, operated from Bridgetown from 1881 to 1938, linking places such as Bath, Martin's Bay, Bathsheba, and Belleplaine. The journey to Bathsheba often took three to four hours, depending on the condition of the railroad, which was sometimes obstructed by landslides.

Upgrading work on a highway. Barbados has about 1,000 miles (1,600 km) of roads.

BARBADIANS

WITH A POPULATION OF 264,400 (1995 ESTIMATE) living on just 166 square miles (430 square km) of land, Barbados is one of the most densely populated countries in the world. More than 70% of Barbadians are direct descendants of slaves from Africa. Another 20% are of mixed black and white heritage, while 7% are white, with traditional Caucasian features and skin tone or with a small amount of black ancestry. The remaining 3% are mostly small immigrant groups from South America and Asia. Barbadians are thus a multi-ethnic people, with Afro-Bajans, Anglo-Bajans of English or Scottish descent, Euro-Bajans, Bajan Jews, Bajan Muslims, Bajan Hindus, and even Arab-Bajans from Syria and Lebanon.

More than half of the population live in the urban region that stretches along the sheltered west coast of the island from Speightstown in the north

Opposite and left: **Today's Barbadians are cheerful and friendly, somewhat reserved around strangers, hospitable to visitors, and proud of their cultural heritage.**

to Oistins in the south and the southeastern parish of St. Philip. The remainder live in numerous villages and hamlets scattered throughout the countryside, ranging in size from 100 to 3,000 people. More than 100,000 people live in the parish of St. Michael alone, the majority of them in the capital city of Bridgetown.

SOCIAL HIERARCHIES

The face of Barbados changed as the original forest cover was replaced by fields of sugarcane and the island became densely settled. The landed elite considered itself an aristocracy. Below the plantocracy in the social structure were hundreds of smaller farming families, traditionally called the yeomanry. Below them was a class of wage laborers, peasants, and unemployed vagrants made up of white indentured servants who had been displaced by black slavery.

Although intermarriages were few, interracial relationships between white planters and black slaves were common. A mulatto population grew on the island, creating a new class of coloreds, who were usually better treated than the blacks. White fathers often had their colored children baptized and freed from slavery.

A wide gap between the very wealthy (white plantocracy) and the very poor (black plantation slaves) has always existed. Although this gap has narrowed since the days of slavery, the contrast between the luxurious mansions of the wealthy and the small chattel houses of the poor remains enormous, as does the difference in lifestyles.

A shell seller.

HIGH WHITES The island's history and economic development has been dominated by about 20 families who still rank among the island's elite today. The great wealth of these families was built on growing sugarcane on huge plantations. The island (which they called Bimshire) was their home, and unlike other West Indian planters, very few were absentee landlords. Instead, they assumed the role of lord of the manor and recreated patterns of English country life. Today, many of their houses bear British names, and they continue to dominate the commercial and economic life of the island.

RED LEGS Before the slave trade brought African blacks to Barbados to work on the sugar plantations, the island's labor force consisted of white indentured servants partly made up of the inmates of English jails and prisoners from the defeated Royalists in the English civil wars.

Whites make up a small minority of the population.

Their contracts were sold to planters on arrival in Barbados where the conditions of their servitude were often no better than slavery. When their indentures ended, some left the island. Those who remained lived in villages on the inhospitable eastern side of the island, where they survived by fishing and hunting turtles and crabs.

Sometimes planters, embarrassed to see them so destitute, provided schools, jobs, and even clubs for them. To keep the poor whites in the city from delinquency, the Young Men's Progressive Club (YMPC) was established in the 1920s. There, they could play cricket, soccer, and indoor games and attend lectures and benefit from cultural programs. The earliest Caribbean literary magazine, *Bim*, was started by Frank Collymore and Therold Barnes, early members of the YMPC and both descendants of poor whites. Today, Bajan poor whites are a small and vanishing minority that is being assimilated completely into the middle class.

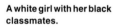

A white girl with her black classmates.

MIXED MARRIAGES

In the past, planters often had a black "outside" woman. Accepting blacks or mulattos socially, however, was another matter, and racial discrimination was practiced in commerce and in the civil service. Today, although attitudes are changing, Bajan whites and blacks do not as a rule marry one another, and most of the interracial couples seen on the island are foreigners.

BAJAN BLACKS

The planters encouraged their African slaves to raise large families, and the population on the island eventually became overwhelmingly Creole. These Creoles gained the reputation of being the most loyal slaves in the West Indies. Nevertheless, the two world wars in the 20th century gave hundreds of Bajan blacks an opportunity to view life from a different perspective overseas. When these Bajan blacks returned home, many helped organize workers and unions to improve their working conditions. The success of blacks in sports, especially cricket, also renewed their pride in their black heritage.

By the 1960s politicians who had spent part of their life abroad were proud to be black and Bajan. Leaders such as Errol Barrow, who had been a World War II airman and trained in London as a lawyer and economist, and Sir Grantley Adams, another London-trained lawyer, worked towards independence for Barbados. Another Bajan black, Sir Winston Scott, who had trained as a doctor in the United States, eventually became the first native governor-general of Barbados in 1967.

A young girl in Bridge-town.

61

NEW BAJANS

The influx of Indians, Pakistanis, and Lebanese, as well as groups from the United States, Canada, England, Germany, South America, and even China has stirred modern Bajan blacks to insist on respect for their hard-won culture. African traditions and folklore have been resurrected, and schoolchildren are encouraged to read the African-inspired poetry of Eddie Braithwaite and the writings of George Lamming, Bruce St. John, and others who have explored in literary form the meanings of being Bajan.

DRESS

Most Barbadians are stylish but conservative in their dress. Women vendors in the marketplaces, for example, often favor old-fashioned, matronly dresses and tie their hair up in handkerchiefs. Office

Barbadians have a great sense of humor.

ALL O'WE IS BAJAN!

The following excerpt from Bruce St. John's *Bumbatuk I* reveals the sense of unity and national pride that exists in Barbados today:

> *All o'we is Bajan!*
> *Bajan to de backbone ...*
> *Bajan black, Bajan white,*
> *Bajan hair curly, Bajan hair straight,*
> *Yo' brother red, yo' sister brown*
> *Yo' mother light-skin, yo' father cob skin ...*

workers, on the other hand, are often seen in tailored dresses or skirts and blouses, and high heels. Skimpy clothes are frowned on in towns and are usually only seen at beach areas.

Even in the most rural areas, schoolchildren, both boys and girls, wear uniforms of pressed shirts and ties, with girls wearing their hair neatly braided and tied with color-coded ribbons. For social events such as weddings and parties, Barbadians love to dress up, and they always wear their Sunday best for church meetings.

SOME PROMINENT BARBADIANS

CRICKETERS One of the world's top players, Bajan national hero Sir Garfield Sobers, was knighted by Queen Elizabeth II during her visit to Barbados in 1975. Sir Frank Worrell, another cricket hero who appears on the face of the Bds$5 bill, was captain of the hugely successful West Indian team that toured Australia in 1960–61. Worrell is buried in a prominently marked grave at the Cave Hill campus of the University of the West Indies.

A woman in traditional dress.

MUSICIANS Calypso artist the Mighty Gabby is famous for his songs on cultural identity and political protest that speak for emerging black pride throughout the Caribbean.

AUTHORS Frank Collymore is regarded as the founder of the Barbadian literary movement. George Lamming is an internationally-recognized novelist and scholar.

LIFESTYLE

CULTURAL INFLUENCES ON BARBADOS, with its British past, are a mixture of African and British heritage. The latter predominates in institutional ways, including the form of government, education, and legal framework, but African influences remain strong in family life and in music and dance.

Supportive networks between female relatives, such as sisters, mothers, and daughters, are especially strong. These networks may sometimes include male relatives such as uncles, brothers, cousins, and grandfathers as well. More than one-third of households in Barbados are headed by women, and the family home remains a place to which Barbadians can return at any time in their lives.

Opposite and left: **Young Barbadians today grow up under a cultural blend of African, British, and more recently, through the power of the media, American influences.**

65

MARRIAGE

Many women enter into a number of different unions before settling down to marriage. Couples may start with a "visiting union," where the woman lives with her parents and is visited by her male friend. Sometimes the couple move in together and eventually marry, but often they remain casual and eventually separate.

Nevertheless, the home and children are the main concerns for most women, and marriage the ultimate goal, even if they have to wait many years. Bajan weddings were once grand affairs with no expense spared. Although elaborate receptions are no longer common because of the rising cost of living, weddings are still important celebrations for Barbadians.

Weddings are usually held in a church on a Saturday afternoon. The bride is usually dressed in white lace, satin, or chiffon and may have as many as eight bridesmaids. The groom and his best man put on stylish, dark suits with orchid boutonnieres.

After the ceremony, the wedding party drives in procession to the reception, where amid speech-making, the couple is toasted and an elaborately-decorated cake is served. This is usually followed by much dancing and feasting until about 11 p.m.

FAMILY LIFE

Couples usually lead relatively separate lives, even engaging in different leisure activities. A father may take an interest in his children's education, but believes his responsibilities are mainly to provide financial support, even if he no longer lives with their mother. Family life is centered around the mother, who performs all the child-rearing tasks. Her relationship with her children is usually close and lasting.

Mothers take their responsibilities seriously, making sure that their children are decently dressed. They are often strict disciplinarians, insisting on good manners and respect for elders. Children are taught to use appropriate greetings when passing people on the road or on entering shops. Three-generation households, especially those consisting of grandmother, mother, and children, are common in Barbados.

Opposite: **A mother and child in Bridgetown.**

Left: **A Barbadian family walks home after attending Sunday service at the local church.**

CHANGING PATTERNS

Today young couples are marrying earlier and both usually continue working. Most will rely on the grandmother to help out with their children, although a fortunate few may be able to afford a maid. Contraception, now generally accepted and easily available, limits the number of children.

DEATH

Grandmothers are often asked to help look after young children when parents go to work.

Religion has always played a significant role in the lives of the people of Barbados. Regardless of their religious affiliation, funeral attendance is considered important by most Bajans.

Funerals start at around 4 p.m. and follow a set ritual. The coffin is placed near the entrance of the church. Close relatives stand on one side, while mourners file past the body. Pamphlets are handed out, detailing hymns to be sung and other procedures to be followed. The coffin is closed and wheeled farther into the church for the service and hymn-singing, prayers, the officiating priest's address, and a eulogy by a close friend of the deceased. As the last church hymn is sung, the coffin is turned around and wheeled feet first to the door. Six pallbearers carry it to the cemetery or into a hearse, which leads a procession of vehicles to the cemetery.

Funerals are attended for a variety of reasons—the deceased might be a relative, neighbor, a casual or job-related acquaintance, or a close friend. Ensuring that the deceased has a good turn out, especially if the death occurred in unusual circumstances, is important. The black and white clothes that were once required wear at funerals have been replaced by lighter colors. Wearing bright colors to a funeral, however, is considered a sign of disrespect. Nowadays, a get-together is usually held after the funeral, during which a variety of food and drink is served. There is no dancing or music, but loud talk and laughter may continue for several hours, serving to relieve temporarily the first-night trauma of the bereaved.

Some Barbadians believe that the dead can convey messages to their kin through dreams. They hold wakes called "nine nights" to ensure that the soul has a safe journey to the next world. They may also conduct ceremonies to communicate with the dead in the hope that the dead will rectify troubles they may have caused while alive.

Funeral services in Barbados are usually well-attended by relatives, friends, and work colleagues.

A neighborhood in Bridgetown.

HOUSING

Some 70% of houses in Barbados are owner-occupied. Almost all households have running water, 80% have televisions and refrigerators, and 55% have telephones. Modern houses are often built from concrete. Many new residential estates for the middle class have sprung up, where satellite dishes and solar panels on the roof are not unusual.

Chattel houses can still be found in many parts of the island. These are houses that were originally designed so that they could be taken apart and moved, if necessary, as slaves were not allowed to own land. The foundations usually consist of stones and the walls of the houses are weathered planks. Traditionally, each window had three wooden shutters (called jalousies), two hinged at the sides and one hinged from above to allow for flexibility in adjusting to sun and wind. Some chattel houses look weather-beaten and neglected, while others have been given a fresh coat of brightly-colored paint.

Barbados also has several plantation houses, most of which have been taken over by the Barbados National Trust. The lifestyle that created these grand homes no longer exists on the island and the houses are now mainly of historical interest.

St. Nicholas Abbey in the parish of St. Peter is the oldest house on the island and one of only three remaining examples of Jacobean architecture in the Americas. The house is believed to have been built in the 1650s. The interior, filled with beautiful antiques and paintings, offers a glimpse of plantation life during those early years.

Drax Hall in the parish of St. George is another fine example of Jacobean architecture. The plantation, one of the first to cultivate sugarcane on a large scale, is the only estate to have stayed in the same family since the 17th century. Sunbury Plantation House in the parish of St. Philip is now a plantation house-cum-museum, with a unique collection of plantation artifacts and tools, such as antique plows and cane carts, on its grounds.

EDUCATION

Barbadians have one of the highest literacy rates in the world, estimated at 98%. School attendance is compulsory for all children between the ages of 5 and 16, and all government schools, both primary and secondary, are free.

ELEMENTARY SCHOOLS About 28,000 pupils attend the 85 elementary schools in Barbados. Children under 5 go to nursery school. Elementary school pupils graduate to junior school when they reach the age of 11. Regardless of their social and economic background, all elementary schoolchildren receive low-cost meals supplied by the government.

SECONDARY SCHOOLS Some 21,000 students between the ages of 11 and 18 are enrolled in the 22 government secondary schools, where the trend is toward a coeducational system. Another 3,000 students attend government-approved private schools.

A schoolgirl in science class.

SPECIAL SCHOOLS Special schools on the island include two government residential industrial schools, which provide training for slow learners, a school for the deaf, a school for the blind, and the Challenor School for the mentally handicapped.

However, the government plans to phase out these schools and incorporate the students into the mainstream education system using progressive remedial programs.

HIGHER EDUCATION A coeducational teachers' training college, opened in 1948, provides training for graduate and nongraduate teachers. The Samuel Jackman Prescod Polytechnic has over 2,000 students. Training is provided for the electrical, building, and engineering trades, commercial and agricultural studies, and human ecology, which includes cosmetology and home economics. The Barbados Community College offers a wide range of academic, vocational, and technical programs, including fine arts, health sciences, liberal arts, and science.

The government also pays the fees of all Barbadians at the Cave Hill campus of the University of the West Indies, which offers courses in arts, natural sciences, social sciences, and law, as well as advanced education for adults at the Extramural Center. The Cave Hill campus is linked to the university's three other campuses in Jamaica, Trinidad, and Bahamas via a telecommunications network that allows teleconferencing and distance teaching. Barbados also has several secretarial colleges and language institutes.

A primary school class in St. James.

The Queen Elizabeth Hospital in Bridgetown has about 600 beds.

Opposite: **A Rastafarian coconut vendor.**

HEALTH

Barbadians enjoy a high standard of healthcare. Several government polyclinics offer health services, including maternal and child care, family planning, health education, school health services, control of communicable diseases, and environmental health. Sir Winston Scott Polyclinic, the island's largest polyclinic, has facilities for X-ray, yellow fever surveillance, bacteriological analysis, and food testing, as well as an eye clinic and a skin disease center. Treatment and medication at these walk-in polyclinics is free for all Barbadians.

ALTERNATIVE MEDICINE

Although modern medicine has superseded traditional folk cures, many Bajans still turn to the indigenous plants and herbs originally used in teas and cures by the early native migrants and the bush medicine brought over from Africa by their ancestors.

The Rastafarian movement also prefers natural cures, which has extended the range of Barbadian folk medicine. Coconut water, sold by Rastafarians on street corners, is regarded as a preventative and cure for illnesses of the kidney and bladder. Similarly, coconut oil can be rubbed on the head to break up a cold or into the scalp to loosen dandruff two days before washing the hair.

The pawpaw (papaya) has many uses. It helps bowel movement and reduces hypertension or high blood pressure when eaten green, in two small, cooked slices. It can be used to prevent infection by applying several thin slices over a cut and then bandaging into place for two or three days. The cactus-like aloe plant also has many uses. For colds, irritated throat, and constipation, a small piece of the inner pith is swallowed with a pinch of salt. Inside slices can be bandaged onto cuts to aid healing, and for sunburn, one side of a piece of aloe is peeled and the cool inside rubbed over the affected area. It is extremely soothing and can even stop the skin from peeling.

A bitter green brew made from the circee bush is used to reduce fevers and relieve influenza symptoms. Wonder-of-the-world, when chewed with a pinch of salt, is believed to relieve mild attacks of asthma.

RELIGION

IN THE EARLY DAYS, despite an official policy of religious tolerance, Catholics, Jews, and nonconformist Protestants were discriminated against and kept from all seats of political power. Anglican clergymen were an important element in the plantocracy that dominated public life and all civic organizations, fashioning social ideologies based on white, Anglo-Saxon Anglicans. It was not until 1797 that Anglican ministers were allowed to offer slaves some religious training. Later, Anglican religious training became part of the preparation for emancipation.

Today, some 40% of the population is Anglican. Among the remaining population, Methodists, Moravians, and Roman Catholics are also well-represented. In addition, there are over 100 other religions, denominations, and sects in Barbados, including Tie-heads, Rastafarians, Jews, Muslims, and Hindus.

Opposite and left: **The island's main religion, Christianity, continues to play an important role in the lives of many Barbadians today.**

A baptism in St. James.

ANGLICANS

After centuries as the official religion in Barbados, the Anglican Church still enjoys the widest following among Barbadians. Its parish churches once dominated rural life, but this is less true today. Anglicans in Barbados are adherents of the Church in the Province of the West Indies.

OTHER CHRISTIAN FAITHS

METHODISTS The first Methodist missionaries arrived in Barbados in the late 18th century and initially struggled to spread their faith in the face of repression. In 1823 its church was destroyed and proclamations threatening to abolish Methodism were posted in Bridgetown. Led by Ann Gill, however, the Methodists resisted. After the Emancipation Act was passed, Methodist ranks were swelled by the newly-freed slaves. Today, there are over 20 Methodist churches on the island.

MORAVIANS The Moravians are the oldest Protestant Episcopal Church in the world. The church became known for supporting slaves under its leader Benjamin Brookshaw, and in 1816 its members were granted virtual immunity from the terror of the slave revolt. Today, Moravians are predominantly black.

ROMAN CATHOLICS Like the other non-Anglican faiths, the formal practice of Catholicism was suppressed before the 19th century. The first Catholic church in Barbados was built in 1848. Catholics are a small minority on the island.

TIE-HEADS

This indigenous Barbadian religion was founded by Bishop Granville Williams in 1957. His first open-air meeting in Oistins was so successful that he soon established the Jerusalem Apostolic Spiritual Baptist Church. Members wear colorful gowns of different colors symbolizing particular qualities, and all tie cloths around their heads. Lively music is accompanied by foot-stomping, hand-clapping, and dancing.

RASTAFARIANS

The Rastafarian movement began in Jamaica in the 1920s when Marcus Garvey advocated a back-to-Africa ideal and urged his followers to "look to Africa, when a black king shall be crowned, for the day of deliverance is at hand." Then in Ethiopia in 1930, Ras Tafari, who claimed to be a direct descendant of King David and 225th in an unbroken line of Ethiopian kings from the time of Solomon and Sheba, was crowned Emperor Haile Selassie I, "King of Kings, Lord of Lords, and the Conquering Lion of the Tribe of Judah." This last title inspired the dreadlocks and the strutting walk by which Rastafarians became identified.

Introduced in Barbados in 1975, the movement spread quickly and for a time attracted undesirable elements, such as criminals and rebellious youths who used it as an excuse to smoke marijuana. This made the movement unpopular with more conservative Barbadians. In due course, however, the fad died down, and some of the remaining Rastafarians have made names for themselves in the fields of sports and the arts.

A Rastafarian is easily distinguished by his dreadlocks. Ras Tafari's followers stress the need to regain pride in their black heritage by leading peaceful, pious lives engaged in contemplation, at the same time rejecting the white man's world.

Hags are especially
ugly spirits,
usually of planters'
wives, that shed
their skin and
traveled about as
balls of fire. If the
skin was found
and rubbed with
pepper or salt, the
hag would be
unable to reenter it
and would die.

FOLK BELIEFS

The lack of Christian missionaries in the early days enabled slaves to retain African folk beliefs and superstitions, some of which still exist:

- *Obeah* ("oh-BEE-ah"), a form of witchcraft believed to have originated from a West African religion called Obi, is now limited to a small number of people who believe in its power. Come-to-me sauce is an *obeah* potion that makes the woman who administers it irresistibly attractive to her victim. Stay-at-home sauce discourages husbands from straying.
- *Duppies* ("DOO-pees"), or spirits of the dead, are supposed to roam the earth at night. To prevent them from entering homes, herbs are hung in the windows and doorways and sand is scattered around the house. This forces the *duppy* to stop and count each grain, which keeps him busy until daylight. Sprinkling a few drops from a new rum bottle on the ground for the spirits remains a Barbadian tradition. *Duppy* dust—grave dirt or pulverized human bones—is supposed to be fatal when thrown on a victim or put in his food.
- *Conrads* ("KON-rads"), or avenging ghosts, are said to take possession of their victims' bodies and shout nasty things in strange voices.
- *Baccoos* ("bah-KOOS"), bestowers of good or evil depending on the amount of attention they get, are tiny men who often live in bottles.

PLACES OF WORSHIP

In Bridgetown, St. Michael's Anglican Cathedral dates from 1789. The original church, built in 1665 to accommodate 3,000 worshippers, was leveled by a hurricane a century later. The present cathedral seats 1,600. Many island notables are buried in the adjacent churchyard, including Sir Grantley Adams, first premier and head of the West Indies Federation from 1958 to 1962, and his son Tom, who was prime minister from 1976 to 1985.

The Barbados Synagogue in Bridgetown was built in 1654 by Jews from Recife, Brazil. Persecuted by the Dutch, they settled in Barbados and, being skilled in the sugar industry, quickly introduced the crop and passed on their skills to local landowners. The synagogue, destroyed by a hurricane in 1831, was rebuilt in 1833, but abandoned in 1929. The distinctive white building has recently been restored.

In Holetown, St. James Parish Church, just north of the town center, is the site of the region's oldest church. The original church built in 1660 was replaced by a more substantial structure in the mid-19th century, but a few vestiges of the original remain, including a bell inscribed with the name of King William cast in the late 1600s.

Some other places of worship include the Emmanuel Baptist Church, the First Church of Christian Scientists, and the Roman Catholic St. Patrick's Cathedral (all in St. Michael), and the Anglican St. Lawrence, the Methodist Hawthorne Memorial, the Bethlehem Moravian, and the Roman Catholic St. Dominic's (all in Christ Church).

The restored Barbados Synagogue has a simple but handsome interior, with brass chandeliers, a checkerboard marble floor, and a columned ladies' balcony. The Jewish population in Barbados numbers around 60.

LANGUAGE

THE OFFICIAL LANGUAGE OF BARBADOS is English. Bajan, however, is the language of the majority of the people. A combination of spoken African languages and English, Bajan has taken time to mature to its present form. Originally, African expressions were translated literally into English, but pronounced with African intonations. However, the English influence slowly became stronger.

Bajan, like other Caribbean dialects, became known as a "Cinderella language," and for a long time was dismissed as the language of the illiterate, restricted to the kitchen and backyard. However, growing pride in black heritage and the emergence of Barbadian writers, poets, and linguists has proved that Bajan has a beauty of its own.

Opposite: **A customer leaves a bookshop in Bridgetown.**

Left: **A schoolboy completes his homework.**

On the public telephone.

BAJAN

The following poem by Bruce St. John serves as an example:

BAJAN	**ENGLISH**
We' language limit?	*Is our language limited?*
Who language en limit?	*Whose language isn't limited?*
Evah language	*Every language*
Like a big pot o' Bajan soup	*Like a big pot of Bajan soup*
Piece o' yam, piece o' potato	*Piece of yam, piece of potato*
T'ree dumplin', two eddoe	*Three dumplings, two eddoes*
One beet, two carrot	*One beet, two carrots*
Piece o' pig-tail, piece o' beef	*Piece of pig-tail, piece of beef*
Pinch o' salt, dus' o' pepper	*Pinch of salt, dusting of pepper*
An' don' fuget okra	*And don't forget okra*
To add to de flavor	*To add to the flavor*
Boil up, cook up, eat up	*Boil it, cook it all together, eat it up*
An' yuh still wan' rice ...	*And you still want rice ...*

From these comparisons, the following can be deduced:

- In Bajan the same form of pronoun can be used as subject, object, or possessive: "we know," "tell we" (tell us), and "we language" (our language);
- a statement becomes a question only by the use of a different intonation;
- endings such as -ed are left out and, in general, words often have the last letter unpronounced and no "s" need be added to indicate plurality.

There is no "th" sound in Bajan and it can be replaced by any of the following: f, v, t, d, z, or k:

Breathe becomes	*breav*
With	*wit, wid, or wif*
Clothe	*cloze or clove*
Think	*t'ink*
The	*de*
Strengthen	*strengken or strengfen*

Bajans use the present tense even for past actions and express "habitual" actions by saying something "does" happen. Instead of using the word "very," Bajans say something is "pretty, pretty, pretty" or "real p - r - e - t - t - y," with great emphasis placed on the word pretty.

Barbadians in Bridgetown. Bajan is the preferred language when with friends.

Colorful murals can be found throughout the island.

STORYTELLING TRADITION

Bajans love to entertain one another with ghost stories, and myths and legends from African sources are part and parcel of everyday conversation. Folk tales and songs combine legend, history, religion, and local events and can be educational, as they often contain a moral lesson, or are purely entertaining, or sometimes both. The West African "Anancy" folk tales inspired the phrase "nancy story," implying a tall tale or lie. A mother might say to her children, "Don't give me no nancy story!"

The following is a Bajan folk tale: *A sick man visits a metaphysician in Bridgetown. The practitioner explains that pain and illness only exist in the mind and all the sick person has to do to get well is to "affirm and believe" that the pain has gone. The sick man follows the practitioner's advice and recovers his health. When the practitioner asks for his fees, his patient tells him, "Wha' fees? All you have to do is affirm and believe dat you have receive de fees and you have dem."*

GREETINGS AND GESTURES

Barbadians consider it impolite not to greet someone with "good morning," "good afternoon," or "good evening," when passing them on

THE BARBADOS NATIONAL ANTHEM

Lyrics by Irving Burgie

In plenty and in time of need
When this fair land was young
Our brave forefathers sowed the seed
From which our pride is sprung
A pride that makes no wanton boast
Of what it has withstood
That binds our hands from coast to coast
The Pride of Nationhood

We loyal sons and daughters all
Do hereby make it known
These fields and hills beyond recall
Are now our very own
We write our name on history's page
With expectations great
Strict guardians of our heritage
Firm craftsmen of our fate.

The Lord has been the people's guide
For past three hundred years
With him still on the people's side
We have no doubts or fears
Upward and onward we shall go
Inspired, exciting, free
And greater will our nation grow
In strength and unity.

the road or entering a shop. Handshakes and smiles are exchanged on meeting. Sometimes, acquaintances will embrace one another. Bajans often wave their hands to greet a passing friend, while conversing to emphasize a point, or merely to call a passing taxi or bus. Folded arms indicate that complete attention is being given to the matter under discussion, but standing with hands on hips usually shows defiance. Puckered lips producing a "chupse" sound express disgust.

THE PUBLIC LIBRARY

In the early part of the 18th century, it was said that "everything was imported into Barbados except books." In 1777 a Literary Society was established and a Library Association in 1814, but both were private organizations for members only.

In 1847, three years before the first Public Libraries Act was passed in Britain, an act was passed in Barbados establishing a public library and museum on the island. However, the library was considered to be "miserably deficient in every branch of literature" by Greville John Chester, an English author/clergyman who spent some months on the island in 1867–68. The present public library on Coleridge Street, paid for by the Scottish-American philanthropist Andrew Carnegie on condition that it should always be maintained as a free library, was opened in 1904.

The public library in Bridgetown is nearly a hundred years old.

COMMUNICATIONS

Barbados is a modern telecommunications center. It is a major regional operations center for Cable & Wireless (West Indies) Ltd, which provides communication by telegraph, telephone, telex, and facsimile worldwide. A local phone company provides cellular and Internet services. Direct-dialing telephone service to most places in the world is available.

Barbados has its own television station with access to satellite and cable channels, two major radio broadcasting companies, and four radio stations. Daily newspapers include *The Advocate* (established in 1895) and *The Nation*. Regional and international publications are also readily available.

Daily newspapers in Barbados. All news media are free of censorship and government control.

SOME BAJAN PROVERBS

Proverbs expressing folk values are constantly used in Bajan homes. Their commonsense wisdom is intended to instruct or admonish people in matters that occur frequently.

If greedy wait, hot will cool. —	Patience will get you what you want.
One bellyful don' fattan a hog. —	Sustained effort is needed to achieve good results.
Hungry mek cat eat salt. —	Necessity makes people do unusual things.
De sea en' got no back door. —	The sea is not a safe place.
Mek-sure better than cock-sure. —	Making sure is better than taking things for granted.
Every skin teet' en' a laugh. —	Friendly smiles may not be genuine.
Hansome don' put in pot. —	Physical beauty does not provide practical benefits.

ARTS

BARBADIANS ARE PROUD OF THEIR CULTURAL HERITAGE, a pride that is particularly evident in their music. The songs of the island's most famous musician, the Mighty Gabby, for example, are infused with a deep love for his homeland. Barbados also has a rich tradition of arts and crafts, literature, and architecture.

MUSIC

Caribbean music has its roots in African folk music and drumming, with some Spanish, French, and English influences. Reggae and calypso are the two types of music heard most often, with their catchy, singable tunes blaring in minibuses and out of restaurants and beach bars. *Soca* ("SOH-ka"), which blends soul with calypso, is dance music with bold rhythms. Heavy on the bass sounds, *soca* is heard most frequently during carnivals.

Opposite: **Wall murals allow Barbadians to express their artistic creativity.**

Left: **Outdoor musicians draw an audience.**

THE MIGHTY GABBY, KING OF CALYPSO

Gabby, whose real name is Tony Carter, began singing at the age of 6 and placed third in his first calypso competition in his teens. He spent a few years in New York, perfecting his writing and performing skills, and on his return to Barbados became the Barbadian equivalent of Jamaica's Bob Marley. He has also won recognition as Folksinger of the Year and his music speaks for the thousands of Barbadians who see their culture under threat from foreign influence.

In *Culture*, he sings:

> *All o' dem shows pon TV you must agree are not for we*
> *Show me some Castle in My Skin by George Lamming*
> *Instead of that trash like Sanford and MASH*
> *Then we could stare in the face*
> *And show dem we cultural base.*

Many local Christian communities have excellent gospel choirs. An annual festival is held over the Whitsun weekend when singers from the United States, the United Kingdom, and the Caribbean converge on Barbados.

CALYPSO Slave songs were first brought by Africans to the West Indies in the early 1600s. Plantation owners thought that beating drums and other loud instruments could encourage their slaves to revolt, so all such instruments were banned. But music remained a vital part of the Africans' daily life and could not be suppressed. The slaves sang while they worked, celebrated holidays with songs, and sang at funerals. Indigenous music went underground. Even after emancipation in 1838, it remained underground and only survived by becoming folk music.

Calypso, which originated in Trinidad, began influencing Barbadian folk music in the early 20th century. The songs from Trinidad increased both the range of melodies and lyrics, which changed from mere gossip and scandal to include satire and social commentary. However, calypso was not taken seriously and early singers were regarded as comics rather than serious performers. Talented Barbadian performers such as the Mighty Charmer and the Mighty Sugar were forced to move to Trinidad for recognition and to make their records. Eventually, in the 1960s and '70s, a group of white middle-class Barbadians called The Merrymen created a series of hits by combining folk and country music with Bajan calypso.

Contemporary calypso features biting social commentary, political satire, or sexual innuendo. Calypso competitions are now a major part of carnival festivities, with singers competing for the title of "king."

TUK BANDS The "boom-a-tuk, boom-a-tuk" sound given out by the big log drum gives these bands their name. For over one hundred years, tuk (also known as tuck or took) music has been played at picnics, excursions, and on public holidays. It is lively, with an intricate fast beat suggestive of English military bands. Tuk bands travel from village to village playing popular tunes and encouraging the villagers to contribute their own compositions. People dress up in unusual clothes and everyone joins in the dancing and fun. Traditional dancers such as the "tiltman," who performs on very tall stilts, usually accompany tuk bands and solicit contributions from the audience.

STEEL DRUM (STEEL PAN) Originally from Trinidad, the distinctive, melodious sounds of this music have spread throughout the Caribbean, including Barbados. It was created by musicians who took discarded oil drums and hammered out the steel bottom, tuning different sections to specific pitches. Drummers now play together in bands.

Steel pan musicians. Each pan, or drum, is custom designed.

DANCE

It is said that most Bajans can dance before they can walk. When music fills the air, toddlers stand and sway to the rhythm of calypso. Early planters quickly realized that their slaves worked better when they were allowed to enjoy their own form of dancing and music once or twice a week. The dancers shouted, clapped their hands, and chanted, twisting and turning energetically.

In recent years, after formal ballet became available to a larger number of Barbadians, modern dance techniques have developed and folk tales have inspired performances by groups such as the Barbados Dance Theater.

LANDSHIPS

The landship movement developed from early friendly societies—institutions, which, for a small weekly payment, provided insurance for the sick as well as death benefits. Landships provided the working class with a social organization that satisfied their need for cultural expression, as well as providing assistance for workers in times of need. Members of landships were ranked and defined in accordance with the hierarchy of the British Navy. Meetings and parades displayed naval-style drills, uniforms, and disciplines.

Many communities developed their own landships in the 1920s. These competed in displays of discipline, uniform, drill, and other naval rituals. Today there are half a dozen landships and no big occasion in Barbados, from a state funeral to the Crop Over festivities, is complete without landship participation.

A dancer performs at a plantation show for tourists.

94

THEATER

Plantation improvisations called "tea meetings" in the 1600s provided entertainment in the form of individuals reciting passages and spontaneous speeches or performing slapstick skits. Troupes of traveling actors would also give spontaneous open-air performances when their ships came into port. The first mention of theater in Barbados, however, appeared in George Washington's diary when he noted that he attended a presentation of *The Tragedy of George Barnwell* in 1751.

By 1783, a theater called Patagonian, which presented plays including Shakespeare, was facing competition from a rival theater called the New Theater, whose comedies and pantomimes drew large crowds. These audiences were made up exclusively of the white planter class. It was not until after World War II that nonwhites such as the Green Room Players began to stage productions of local and international plays.

Stage One Theater Productions, established in 1979, concentrates on works about the Caribbean way of life. Its production of Errol John's *Moon on a Rainbow Shawl* has been a great success. In the play, the child Esther is talented in needlework and embroidery, but the patterns she creates are not those that her society encourages. She finds her own patterns "prettier, though much harder to do." The shawl she creates becomes a symbol of hope for all the different aspects and identities of the Caribbean territories that have evolved from colonialism toward their independent future.

A modern-day dinner theater production, Barbados by Night, *at the Plantation Restaurant and Garden Theater, provides a whirlwind of dance and energy, depicting the cultures of the Caribbean as influenced by the English, French, Spanish, and Africans. It also features fire-eating limbo dancers, and steelband, reggae, and calypso music.*

DINNER THEATERS

The play *1627 and All That* presented at the Sherbourne Conference Center recreates a 17th century Barbadian ambience. The main event, a dramatization of 17th century Barbadian life, is vividly performed by a troupe of energetic dancers.

ARCHITECTURE

Architecture in Barbados is a blend of British tradition and tropical design, elegance and simplicity. There are grand Georgian, Jacobean, and Victorian buildings on the one hand and basic wooden houses of the early settlers and slaves on the other. The wealth of the large sugar plantations resulted in the construction of great houses—solid structures built from natural coral limestone and furnished with mahogany furniture.

Speightstown retains its early architecture. Bridgetown's colonial buildings on Broad Street exemplify the grandeur and architectural flourishes of the turn of the century, but they are now increasingly being surrounded by more modern structures. The public buildings with neo-Gothic facades, erected in the 19th century on the northern side of Trafalgar Square, accommodate the Houses of Parliament.

TYROL COT HERITAGE VILLAGE

Constructed in 1854 by a local builder, William Farnum, the Tyrol Cot Great House is a restrained blend of Palladian and tropical design. The home of Sir Grantley Adams for 60 years, it is filled with his collection of antique furniture and memorabilia.

The chattel houses of the Heritage Village display the work of craftsmen and artists who work on site. The houses are built of traditional materials and incorporate many carefully reproduced details, such as gingerbread trim, verandah lattice work, and wooden shutters.

CHATTEL HOUSES

These simple, rectangular wooden homes—built on cement or stone blocks so that they could be moved—are often painted in original combinations of vivid colors such as turquoise, lime, pink, and yellow. They are a favorite subject for culture-preserving painters such as Fielding Babb, Adrian Compton, the Stewart twin brothers, the Cumberbatch twin sisters, and Oscar Walkes.

Karl Broodhagen has become perhaps the best-known sculptor and painter in Barbados. Many famous Barbadians, including Sir Grantley Adams, have been immortalized in bronze by him, but the Emancipation Statue, commemorating the 150th anniversary of emancipation, is perhaps his most outstanding work.

ARTS AND CRAFTS

It is difficult to distinguish between arts and crafts in Barbados. For centuries, artists and craftsmen have turned functional things into works of art by decorating simple everyday objects.

The Temple Yard Rastafarian community of craftsmen produces various items made from leather, clay, wood, and even straw. Akyem, who is a master of clay, produces plaques, low-relief scenes, and sculptures.

The island's chief showcase for handicrafts is Pelican Village near Bridgetown Harbor, which has galleries and workshops where craftsmen can display their products, including coconut shell accessories, straw fans, bottle baskets, and mahogany objects such as key rings, jewelry boxes, ashtrays, coaster sets, and letter boxes. Pottery, wall hangings, woven baskets of all shapes, mats, rugs, and shell and coral jewelry are also featured.

CHALKY MOUNT POTTERIES In the parish of St. Andrew stands a hill of stratified clays of different colors —red, yellow, brown, and white—sandwiched between a thin strata of shale. For centuries, this was the source of material for making household items such as lamps and candlestands, cups, plates, and bowls, as well as the clay pots used as stoves in many homes and the jugs called "monkeys" designed to cool beverages. The potter's craft has been handed down in families from generation to generation. Courtney Devonish, originally from Chalky Mount, has a gallery-cum-workshop in Pelican Village. Trained in Italy, he is able to create classic European styles as well as traditional island pottery.

Pottery display at Chalky Mount.

ORNATE MURALS Local communities and schoolchildren are encouraged by the Cultural Foundation to create murals that depict cultural, historical, and social aspects of their neighborhoods, as well as popular local characters. Such colorful representations of present-day Bajan daily life can be found on the walls of schools, community centers, and post offices.

REVELATION

H. A. Vaughn's *Revelation*, dedicated to the black woman, is the most quoted poem to emerge from Barbados:

> Turn sideways now and let them see
> What loveliness escapes the schools,
> Then turn again, and smile, and be
> The perfect answer to those fools
> Who always prate of Greece and Rome
> "The face that launched a thousand ships"
> And such like things, but keep tight lips
> For burnished beauty nearer home.
> Turn in the sun, my love, my love!
> What palm-like grace! What poise! I swear
> I prize these dusky limbs above
> My life. What laughing eyes! What gleaming hair!

Storytelling, for centuries a traditional way for Bajans to entertain each other and pass on folk traditions, has taken on an additional form today—local radio broadcasts of stories that focus on Barbadian culture and village life.

LITERATURE

The island's high literacy rate has produced several respected novelists and poets who blended folk beliefs with their own experiences, creating a rich literary tradition. In the 1940s the British Broadcasting Corporation radio program *Caribbean Voices* and Barbadian magazine *Bim*, edited by Frank Collymore, first brought to public notice writers such as George Lamming, Oliver Jackman, Derek Walcott, Monica Skeete, and others who later authored highly-acclaimed novels and poetry.

Many early Bajan novels dealt with childhood, the coming of age, the search for self in an world of color and race, bondage, and freedom. George Lamming's *In the Castle of My Skin*, *The Emigrants*, and *Season of Adventure*, in which a mulatto woman searches for the meaning and value of her life when voodoo drums send her into a frenzy, have become classics. Geoffrey Drayton's *Christopher* deals with a white Bajan boy growing up in a black society, while Austin Clarke's *Amongst Thistles and Thorns* is the reverse—a black Bajan boy coming to terms with a white society.

LEISURE

BARBADIANS AND VISITORS ALIKE find the island a perfect setting for a great variety of sports and other leisure activities. Barbadians love to play, relax, and entertain themselves, and if they cannot afford the costly equipment required for some sports, they are happy to turn to pursuits that can be enjoyed inexpensively. The most popular sport in Barbados is cricket.

CRICKET

Cricket was introduced about 200 years ago by the British military who regularly held cricket matches at the Garrison Savannah. It soon became popular with white planters and merchants who set up their own clubs and organized matches. Cricket was considered to be character-building and to reflect the nobler values of British culture.

Opposite: **A catamaran approaches the beach. Water sports are a popular pastime in Barbados.**

Left: **Children enjoy a game of basketball.**

Barbadians take up cricket at a young age. Many hope one day to play for the West Indies team that selects its players from the best in the Caribbean.

In the early days the clubs such as The Wanderers (formed in 1877 by members of the mercantile community) and The Pickwick (formed by members of the plantocracy) were strictly white. Black and mixed-race professionals formed their own club, Spartan, whose members blackballed Herman Griffith, a public health inspector, because he was considered to be socially beneath them. Griffith's supporters broke away and formed the Empire Club, and Griffith became one of the great players of the game and the first black captain of a Barbados team. These four clubs are still active, but the structure of their membership has changed.

Early cricket was centered around Bridgetown and confined to a comparatively small portion of the population. Nevertheless, artisans and other workers soon formed their own clubs. Recognizing the game's potential for building community spirit, plantation employers encouraged their workers to play cricket by providing them with land for a pitch and handing down second-hand kit and equipment no longer needed by their own clubs. These lesser teams arranged their own competitions and rivalry was intense.

When the Barbados Cricket League was formed, it brought the different groups of cricketers together in a way which made them realize that plantation owners and business executives could find camaraderie and respect for the black civil servants and lawyers they played against. Cricket can thus be said to have paved the way to independence.

When Barbados became independent in 1966, it challenged the rest of the world to a showcase cricket match. It remains one of the international capitals of cricket and always contributes a large contingent to the West Indies team.

Cricket is played at top-level international test matches between January and April, when Kensington Oval is filled to its 15,000 capacity. The Cricket Association and the Cricket League also manage to pack a hundred matches into the limited schedule available on Saturday afternoons during a season lasting from early June to mid-September.

Bridgetown-born Garfield Sobers is widely acknowledged to be one of the world's greatest ever cricket players. He represented the West Indies 93 times from 1954–74.

Friendly matches are played on beaches, open pastures, or village fields all year round. Young boys who dream of escaping from poverty and making a name for themselves know that mastering cricket could mean more to their future than any other skill. As a result, they play cricket anywhere, anytime.

OTHER SPORTS

SOFTBALL Using tennis balls instead of leather balls, and slim mahogany bats instead of regulation willow bats from England, this modified form of cricket is played on Sunday mornings when more than 100 softball teams compete for places on the Barbados teams that regularly tour the United States and Canada.

RUNNING Long-distance running is a popular activity in Barbados. All over the island, men and women walking briskly or jogging have become a common sight. An annual Run Barbados International Road Race is held the first weekend in December. The 26 mile 385 yard (42.2 km) marathon over paved roads along the coast and in and around Bridgetown attracts male and female competitors from around the world.

Every evening, the Savannah Garrison in Bridgetown is taken over by joggers who circle the track at various speeds.

DOMINOES This game, played with such enthusiasm that the slap of the dominoes on the table can be startling, is the national table game. It even has a festival in June when the world's top dominoes players come to compete in the World Dominoes Festival.

GOLF Four golf courses and fine weather all year round help make Barbados a popular golfing destination. The versatile cricket legend Sir Garfield Sobers has also captained the Barbados golf team.

WATER SPORTS Constant sunshine and steady breezes on the southern coast produce ideal conditions for windsurfing. At the Soup Bowl, a bay near Bathsheba, waves from the Atlantic Ocean and clean, shark-free waters create equally ideal conditions for surfers.

Yachting is another popular sport. Coral reefs and sunken wrecks in clear water surrounding the island also provide scuba diving enthusiasts with excellent diving sites.

Scuba divers off St. James. Most beach resorts have facilities for jet skis and water skiing. Parasailing is another popular pastime.

NATIONAL PARKS

Several national parks on the island have become popular recreation areas for both Barbadians and visitors. Perhaps the most well-known, Farley Hill National Park, consists of several acres of tropical trees and plants on a cliff 900 feet (275 m) above sea level, overlooking the Scotland District. Bought by the Barbados government and declared a national park, it was officially opened by Queen Elizabeth II on February 15, 1966, just several months before the island's independence.

The original mansion in the park was built on the grand scale of 19th century plantation houses. After the owner Thomas Graham Briggs died

A couple enjoy the scenery at one of Barbados's national parks.

in 1887, the mansion lost its elegance. Even so, Hollywood moviemakers chose it for the Fleury home, Belfontaine, for the movie of Alex Waugh's novel *Island in The Sun*. In 1956 the crumbling old palace was transformed at enormous cost into a mansion worthy of a sugar baron. A new gallery and stairway was built, and a new open verandah was added in front of the main entrance, where an artificial lake was constructed. Unfortunately, a few years later, a great fire destroyed everything except the walls.

RUM SHOPS

Gatherings of family and friends for Sunday lunches are a favorite weekend activity. However, get-togethers on Sunday mornings at the island's numerous rum shops to discuss topics ranging from politics to cricket are even more popular with men.

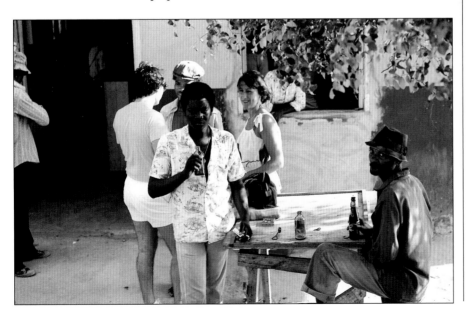

Patrons at a rum shop. The rum shop becomes a men's club and meeting place on weekends for lively discussions.

FESTIVALS

BESIDES RELIGIOUS HOLIDAYS SUCH AS EASTER AND CHRISTMAS, Barbadians look forward to six major events in the festive calendar every year. These festivals are the Jazz Festival (held in January), Holetown Festival (from February 17), Oistins Fish Festival (Easter weekend), De Congaline Carnival (from April 23), Crop Over Festival (from mid-June), and the National Independence Festival of Creative Arts (throughout November).

A number of sports festivals, such as the Mount Gay International Regatta (January), Mountain Bike Festival (February), International Netball Clubs Festival (June), Banks Hockey Festival (August), as well as several cricket festivals, are also held throughout the year.

Opposite: **A participant in the Crop Over Festival, a highlight of the cultural calendar.**

Left: **Spectators at Independence Day celebrations in Bridgetown.**

JAZZ FESTIVAL

In January top-class performers from all over the world come to Barbados to provide a weekend of the best jazz talents against a backdrop of tropical splendor.

HOLETOWN FESTIVAL

The site of the landing of the first permanent settlers on February 17, 1627, is the setting for a week of continuous entertainment each year. Medieval songs are sung in churches, while more modern beats can be heard in the fairgrounds. Jazz, gospel, brass, and folk concerts are held by the light of the moon on the beach where the first 80 settlers landed nearly 400 years ago.

Young Barbadians take a break from the festivities of the Holetown Festival. A major street parade takes place on the final weekend when Holetown becomes the setting for a two-day street market featuring stalls offering handicrafts and traditional Bajan, Caribbean, and international foods.

OISTINS FISH FESTIVAL

Held over the Easter weekend, this festival pays tribute to the island's fishing folk, who hold competitions over several days to demonstrate their skills in fishing, fish-deboning, boat racing, and even crab racing. Spectators mingle with the crowds thronging the beaches, market places, and rum shops that line the roadsides and dance to steel bands.

DE CONGALINE CARNIVAL

Ten days of festivities begin on April 23. Celebrations climax on May 1 with the massive May Day parade, when thousands dance to hot calypso rhythms. Live musical performances run during the days in between, and Barbados's only steel band competition is one of the major attractions. The De Congaline Festival has been celebrated since the early 1990s.

CROP OVER FESTIVAL

Originally, plantation managers held a "dinner and sober dance" to celebrate harvest time. Before emancipation, planters had to support their slaves all year round, but after 1838, Crop Over meant less work and lower wages and, for many workers, a period of hard times. The figure of a man stuffed with trash from the sugarcane plant became known as Mr. Harding. Workers would parade around the plantation yards in their carts with their animals decorated with flamboyant frangipani and other flowers. After introducing Mr. Harding to the manager, they would adjourn for dancing and food, with salted meat and rum being contributed by the manager.

By 1940 Crop Over as a custom had virtually died out. However, it was revived in 1974 to pay tribute to the vital role of sugar in Barbados's history. Perhaps the most elaborate and important festival, Crop Over lasts for five weeks from mid-June to August. The Ceremonial Delivery of the Last Canes opens the festivities and is followed over the next few weeks by attractions such as a decorated cart parade and a calypso competition.

The grand finale of Crop Over, Kadooment Day, is marked by a carnival parade around the National Stadium in Bridgetown that then moves out onto the streets.

111

Costume designers compete for the coveted best designer award in the Kadooment Day carnival parade.

The Cohobblopot variety show, which blends drama, dance, and music with the crowning of the king and queen of the costumed bands, is another major draw. The massive Bridgetown market street fair offers selections of Bajan cooking and local arts and crafts. The king of calypso is crowned at the Pic-o-de-Crop Show. The climax of the festival is Kadooment Day on the first Monday in August, which is a national holiday. Revelers dress up in spectacular costumes and dance along the streets in a huge carnival parade to the most popular calypso and soca sounds. At the end of the route, a lively fete takes place with more music, color, fun, and food.

NATIONAL INDEPENDENCE FESTIVAL OF CREATIVE ARTS

Bajans of all ages match their talents in music, singing, dancing, acting, and writing during the festival. Performances by the finalists are held on Independence Day—November 30.

BARBADOS'S PUBLIC HOLIDAYS

New Year's Day	January 1
Errol Barrow Day	January 21
Good Friday & Easter Monday	late March/early April
May Day	May 1
Whit Monday	eighth Monday after Easter
Kadooment Day	first Monday in August
United Nations Day	first Monday in October
Independence Day	November 30
Christmas Day	December 25
Boxing Day	December 26

FOOD

BARBADOS OFFERS AN ENORMOUS VARIETY of gastronomic delights, including spicy Bajan and Caribbean specialties. Some of these dishes borrow heavily from African, Indian, or even Chinese sources.

TRADITIONAL FOODS

COU-COU AND SALT FISH African-inspired, *cou-cou* ("koo-koo") is considered the Bajan national dish. A mixture of corn meal and okra is stirred vigorously to prevent lumps, packed into a bowl, and then turned out onto a plate. A depression is made in the center of the pudding and a sauce is ladled into this and around the mound.

Cou-cou is traditionally served with salt fish. Originally imported to feed the slaves because it was an inexpensive source of protein, salt fish is now regarded as a delicacy.

Opposite: **A fruit market in Bridgetown.**

Left: **A chef at work.**

FLYING FISH AND OTHER SEAFOOD Virtually a national symbol, the flying fish is perhaps the most popular Bajan delicacy. Caught between December and June, it is frozen or dried for use during the rest of the year. It can be prepared in many ways, from beachside sandwiches (called fish cutters) to gourmet dishes. Fresh from the surrounding waters come other seafood, such as lobster, shrimp, dorado, turtle, red snapper, tuna, king fish, and mackerel. Unique are the crane chubb and sea eggs (white sea urchins' roe deviled, breaded, or prepared to taste).

A flying fish burger.

STEW FOOD Barbadians love pork and every bit of the pig is used in some way. Traditionally cooked midweek when fresh or more expensive foods run out, stew food is made from finely chopped pig's tail, snout, head, and trotters. It is cooked with green vegetables, such as okra, squash, cabbage, or spinach, and served with ground provisions—root vegetables such as yams, sweet potatoes, and cassava—as well as breadfruit.

PUDDING AND SOUSE Pudding, which resembles a long dark sausage, is made from grated, well-seasoned sweet potato stuffed into a cleaned pig's intestine and steamed. The sausage is then cut into slices and served with souse made from pork—including the head and the trotters—cooked, sliced, and soused (pickled) with lime juice, onion, hot peppers, salt, chopped cucumber, and parsley. This dish is a traditional Saturday night meal when the family gets together. Leftovers are usually fried and served for breakfast the following day.

FRUITS AND VEGETABLES

Barbados's tropical climate yields fruits such as mangoes, papayas, bananas, guavas, avocados, and coconuts in abundance. Other fruits eaten include Barbados cherries and the soursop—a large green fruit with a slightly acidic, pulpy texture that is often made into a refreshing drink. Breadfruit is a staple in the Bajan diet. The size of a melon, breadfruit has white starchy and slightly spongy flesh that can be cooked in stews or fried, boiled, or pickled.

Also abundant are vegetables such as yams, eggplant, okra, pumpkin, plantains (resembling large bananas, this starchy fruit is usually fried or grilled and eaten as a vegetable accompaniment to other dishes), squash, and christophenes—a common Caribbean vegetable shaped like a large pear that can be eaten raw in salads, used in soups, or cooked like squash.

A Barbadian dish of fish, chicken, breadfruit, and mango.

OTHER BAJAN SPECIALTIES

Some other popular Bajan dishes include:
- Jug-jug, a mixture of Guinea corn, green peas, and salted meat
- Pepperpot, a spicy stew made with a variety of meats
- *Roti* ("ROW-tee"), a curry filling of meat or chicken and potatoes wrapped in a tortilla-like flat bread
- Conkies, a mixture of corn meal, coconut, pumpkin, raisins, sweet potatoes, and spices, steamed in a plantain leaf

SUNDAY BUFFETS

The Bajan custom of entertaining family and friends on the weekend is still popular, and Sunday buffets in particular provide a good excuse for festive parties with plentiful food, drink, and music.

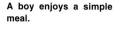

A boy enjoys a simple meal.

STREET THAT NEVER SLEEPS

In Bridgetown, Baxter Road becomes an ongoing party every night when rum shops and restaurants open their doors and music and wonderful aromas fill the air. At one end, vendors stand over buckpots, or old cast-iron pots, deep-frying fish, chicken, or pork Bajan-style over bright coal fires. Locals and visitors mingle, eating and drinking until the early hours of the morning.

COCONUT BREAD

A Bajan favorite that can be served plain or lightly buttered is made from the following ingredients:

6 oz (170 g) brown sugar
6 oz (170 g) shortening
1 large egg
3 cups grated coconut
1 teaspoon each powdered cinnamon & nutmeg
2 teaspoons almond extract
1¼ lb (0.6 kg) raisins or mixed fruits
1 cup milk
1¼ lb (0.6 kg) flour
3 teaspoons baking powder
½ teaspoon salt

Cream together the sugar and shortening. Beat the egg well, then add into the sugar/shortening mixture. Next, add the grated coconut, spices, almond extract, raisins, and milk. Sift the flour with salt and baking powder and mix it in. Fill a greased 3 lb (1.35 kg) loaf pan with the mixture and bake in an oven at 375°F (140°C) for about an hour, or until the bread is golden brown. Cool on a rack before serving.

A bartender at the Mount Gay Rum visitors' center.

DRINKS

RUM Rum is the social drink of Barbados. It is drunk at weddings, births, christenings, wakes, and funerals, as well as on any other occasion that provides a reason for celebrating. It may be drunk straight from a bottle passed from hand to hand, with ice, or diluted with fruit juices in the form of delicious rum punches.

When it was first made in the 1640s by distilling the juice extracted from molasses (the thick liquid residue left after most of the sugar has been taken out of the sugarcane juice), rum was not as refined as it is today. Then, it was called rumbullion or kill-devil because it was so potent. Planters sold their rum to ships for consumption by the crews and resale overseas and to the taverns that sprang up all over the island and later became rum shops. Rum was in great demand and helped to make the planters prosperous.

There are nearly one thousand rum shops on the island today. These shops have become much more than just shops selling rum. Functioning more like a village store selling groceries and fuel, they are informal community centers where men meet to exchange "gup and gossip," discuss politics, or simply hang out. Women rarely frequent rum shops and then only if with a male escort.

Among internationally recognized brands, Mount Gay Rum claims to be the oldest in the Caribbean, and possibly the world. A legal document dated February 29, 1703, lists "two stone windmills, one boiling house with seven coppers, one curing house, and one still house" (all equipment essential for the making of rum) on the estate that was renamed Mount Gay to honor Sir John Gay Alleyne after he died in 1801.

High quality sugarcane and crystal pure water are the basic ingredients for making rum. Single and double distillations of the spirit are produced and stored in charred oak barrels that are left to age in cellars for various lengths of time, eventually to be married (blended) by a master blender in accordance with secret recipes.

Selling drinks in Bridgetown.

BEER AND OTHER DRINKS The island beer, Banks, is popular with both locals and visitors. Other popular drinks include coconut water, fresh lemonade, and punches made from the juices of fruits such as mangoes, guavas, soursops, passion fruit, and tamarinds.

Mauby is made by boiling bits of bitter bark (*Colubrina elliptica*) with spices. It is then strained and sweetened. Sorrel, the local Christmas drink, is prepared from the fresh or dried red sepals of the sorrel plant, which are boiled or infused in hot water with spices and rum added. Falernum is a local liqueur made with lime juice, granulated sugar, rum, and water that has been flavored with almond extract.

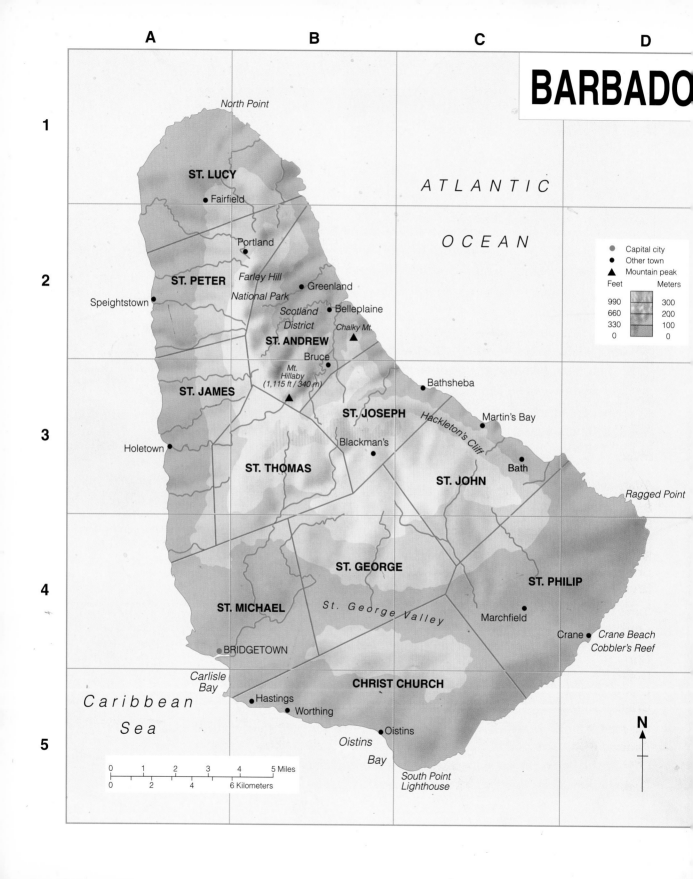

BARBADO

A   B   C   D

1

North Point

ST. LUCY

● Fairfield

Portland ●

ST. PETER

Farley Hill
National Park

● Greenland

Speightstown ●

Scotland
District

● Belleplaine

Chalky Mt. ▲

ST. ANDREW

Bruce ●

Mt.
Hillaby
(1,115 ft / 340 m) ▲

ST. JAMES

● Bathsheba

ST. JOSEPH

Hackleton's Cliff

● Martin's Bay

Holetown ●

Blackman's ●

● Bath

ST. THOMAS

ST. JOHN

Ragged Point

ST. GEORGE

ST. PHILIP

ST. MICHAEL

St. George Valley

Marchfield ●

Crane ● *Crane Beach*
Cobbler's Reef

● BRIDGETOWN

Carlisle
Bay

CHRIST CHURCH

C a r i b b e a n
S e a

● Hastings
● Worthing

● Oistins

Oistins
Bay

South Point
Lighthouse

ATLANTIC

OCEAN

● Capital city
● Other town
▲ Mountain peak

Feet   Meters
990   300
660   200
330   100
0   0

N

0   1   2   3   4   5 Miles
0   2   4   6 Kilometers

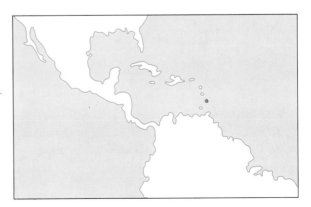

QUICK NOTES

AREA
166 square miles
(430 square km)

POPULATION
264,400 (1995 official estimate)

CAPITAL
Bridgetown

OFFICIAL NAME
Barbados

OFFICIAL LANGUAGE
English

HIGHEST POINT
Mount Hillaby (1,115 feet / 340 m)

MAIN RELIGION
Christianity (mainly Anglican)

CLIMATE
Tropical

NATIONAL FLOWER
Pride of Barbados

MAJOR TOWNS
Speightstown, Holetown

PARISHES
St. Michael, Christ Church, St. Philip, St. George, St. John, St. Joseph, St. Thomas, St. James, St. Andrew, St. Peter, St. Lucy

NATIONAL FLAG
Three equal vertical stripes of blue, gold, and blue, with the head of a black trident superimposed in the center of the gold band

CURRENCY
The Barbados dollar
1 dollar = 100 cents
US$1 = B$2

MAIN EXPORTS
Sugar and molasses, electrical/electronic components, clothing, chemicals

MAJOR IMPORTS
Machinery, food and beverages, fuels, automobiles

POLITICAL LEADERS
Sir Grantley Adams—first premier in 1954
Errol W. Barrow—first prime minister in 1966
Owen S. Arthur—prime minister since 1994

MAIN POLITICAL PARTIES
Barbados Labor Party (BLP)
Democratic Labor Party (DLP)
National Democratic Party (NDP)

PROMINENT BARBADIANS
Sir Garfield Sobers, The Mighty Gabby, Frank Collymore

ANNIVERSARY
Errol Barrow Day (January 21)
Independence Day (November 30)

GLOSSARY

Arawaks
Early inhabitants of Barbados, who originally came from South America.

baccoo ("bah-KOO")
Tiny man who bestows good or evil, depending on the amount of attention he receives.

Bajan
A term used to describe the people of Barbados or Barbadians.

Caribs
An aggressive tribe of native peoples who settled in the Caribbean islands, including Barbados, displacing the Arawaks.

casareep ("ka-sa-REEP")
An original Arawak flavoring made from grated, ground cassava still used in cooking today.

chattel houses
Moveable dwellings.

conkies
A mixture of cornmeal, coconut, pumpkin, raisins, sweet potatoes, and spices, steamed in a plaintain leaf.

conrad ("KON-rad")
Avenging ghost.

cou-cou ("koo-koo")
Popular Bajan dish made from a mixture of cornmeal and okra.

duppy ("DOO-pee")
Spirit of the dead who roams at night.

duppy dust
Grave dirt or pulverized human bones that can kill if thrown on a victim.

hags
Ugly spirits, usually of planters' wives, that shed their skin and travel about as balls of fire.

high whites
Descendants of the elite planter families who still control much of Barbados's commercial life.

jug-jug
Dish of corn, green peas, and salted meat.

obeah ("oh-BEE-ah")
A form of witchcraft.

parish
Unit of local administration.

plantocracy
Wealthy planter class.

red legs
Descendants of white indentured servants.

soca ("SOH-ka")
A form of dance music with bold rhythms and heavy bass sounds frequently played during carnivals.

BIBLIOGRAPHY

Beckles, Hilary. *A History of Barbados*. Cambridge: Cambridge University Press, 1990.

Broberg, Merle. *Places and Peoples of the World: Barbados*. New York: Chelsea House, 1989.

Forde, G. Addington, Sean Carrington, Henry Fraser, and John Gilmore. *The A–Z of Barbadian Heritage*. Bridgetown: Heinemann Caribbean, 1990.

Handler, Jerome S. *Plantation Slavery in Barbados*. Cambridge: Harvard University Press, 1978.

Lamming, George. *In the Castle of My Skin*. London: Schocken, 1983.

Puckrein, G.A. *Little England: Plantation Society & Anglo-Barbadian Politics 1627–1700*. New York: New York University Press, 1984.

INDEX

INDEX

INDEX